P9-EMN-598

NEW LAW AND LIFE

60 PRACTICAL QUESTIONS AND ANSWERS ON THE NEW CODE OF CANON LAW

EDITED BY ELISSA RINERE, C.P., J.C.L.

Originally Syndicated by
The Catholic Transcript
Hartford, Connecticut

© Copyright 1985 by the Canon Law Society of America

Canon Law Society of America
Washington, DC 20064
ISBN: 0-943616-28-X

FOREWORD

Law is intended for the life of people. John XXIII sensed this when he called for an updating of church law. John Paul II also recognized this truth when he issued the revised code in 1983. But more importantly, the people of the Church know it by their practical living of the discipline of the Church.

Lawyers, including church lawyers (or, canon lawyers) have the ministry of aiding the people of the Church live out their lives in unity and solidarity, a communion carrying on the mission Christ entrusted to His followers. This community is served and led by their pastors who bear a great responsibility for the faith, life and discipline of the Church.

As an aid to people and pastors alike, the Canon Law Society of America undertook in 1983 to provide a column in the Catholic press to assist in understanding the revised code. Sister Elissa Rinere, C.P., of the Tribunal of the Archdiocese of Hartford generously headed up the project, ably assisted by the members of the Society who volunteered to write individual columns at her request. The *Catholic Transcript* of Hartford syndicated the column, which has been carried by nearly thirty Catholic papers in the United States.

The present booklet reproduces the questions raised by Catholics in the United States and the responses published in the CLSA column. Each article is the work of an individual canonist, identified at the conclusion of the column. The opinions expressed in these articles are those of the author, and carry only the authority of the person who wrote the article.

The CLSA is pleased to make these materials available in booklet form as part of its continuing commitment to further the pastoral life of the people of God in whatever ways are appropriate under the heading of canon law.

JAMES H. PROVOST
CLSA EXECUTIVE COORDINATOR

CONTENTS

Introduction

Sacraments and Sacred Rites

Marriage and Annulment

Catholic People and Catholic Practice

Church Structures and Operations

Last Word

1. WHAT AND WHY?

What is a code *of law?*

A code of law is a systematic collection of legislation. As all law, it governs the behavior of a specific group of people and provides for order within the group. Unlike other systems of legislation, however, a code is formulated and presented as a unit; it is all inclusive, usually having no mechanism for easy or automatic change and updating. There are many examples of codified legal systems in history.

The Church was given its first code of law in 1917. It was called for by Pope Pius X as an improvement over the many church laws which were somewhat unorganized and, therefore, unavailable to many. This codified legal system had a great impact on the Church, giving new clarity and accessibility to legal principles.

Why is the law of the Church called Canon Law?

The name "canon law" comes from the actual form in which the law is presented to those who read it. The word "canon" comes from a Greek word which means rule or norm. Thus, the law of the Church is a series of rules or norms which govern the life of the community—a law which is a series of canons. The name canon law has been given to the law of the Church since the 12th century.

Why is there a new Code of Canon Law for the Church?

The 1917 code was a systematic and useful text for legal matters in church life. It was also, however, a product of its time. Since the code had no built in mechanism for revision, as times changed it became outdated. In 1959, when the code was more than 40 years old, Pope John XXIII called for a renewal of the Church through Vatican Council II and for a revision of the 1917 Code of Canon Law.

The commission which did the rewriting was established in 1963 and its work took 20 years to complete. There was much discussion and world-wide consultation during these years, resulting in the 1983 Code of Canon Law which attempts to incorporate the principles of Vatican II into the legal structure of the Church.

ELISSA RINERE, C.P.

2. BAPTISM BY DEACON

My grandchild was recently baptized and the ceremony was done by our neighbor who is a deacon. Can he do this? Wasn't a priest supposed to baptize the baby?

We all know, of course, that one of the seven sacraments is holy orders and that there are three orders: bishop, priest, and deacon. These three orders find their roots in the earliest days of the Church's life and together they form the basic structure of ordained ministry in the Church. Most people are familiar with the role and function of bishops and priests. The role of deacons, on the other hand, is a bit more "mysterious."

Throughout the history of the Church and until modern times, deacons had many duties and privileges in the Church. In addition to baptizing, preaching, and assisting at the altar, deacons often acted as officials and counselors of popes and bishops. In fact, until 1917, when the first Code of Canon Law was published, deacons could be appointed pastors of parishes. However, for various historical and theological reasons, deacons lost most of these functions and, in effect, the diaconate became just the final major step toward ordination to the priesthood.

The Second Vatican Council has changed all that. One of the many changes brought about by the council was the restoration of the permanent diaconate as a full and proper ministry in the Church. Thus, we now have in the Church two kinds of deacons, permanent and transitional. As the very terms suggest, transitional deacons are deacons who are preparing to be ordained priests and thus their diaconate is of a relatively short duration (6 months to a year). Permanent deacons, however, are not preparing for the priesthood. These deacons are very often married and serve the Church usually on a part-time basis.

Therefore, in answer to your question, children can be baptized by deacons. The 1983 Code of Canon Law says this clearly: "The ordinary minister of baptism is the bishop, priest and deacon . . ." (canon 861, §1). In addition to baptizing, deacons can preach, assist at the altar, and perform other functions designated by the bishop.

Thus, the deacon who baptized your grandchild was acting in accord with the role given him by church law.

MICHAEL H. GOSSELIN

3. REFUSAL OF BAPTISM

My daughter and her husband are Catholic but do not go to Mass. The pastor of their parish has refused to baptize their child. How can a priest do this?

This is obviously a painful and complex situation. There are a number of issues involved here which need to be carefully appreciated.

In general, it is necessary to keep in mind that Vatican II brought about a new and richer understanding of the sacraments. Briefly put, there is now much more attention given to the proper disposition and preparation for the sacraments as well as a renewed emphasis on the role of the whole community of faith. In other words, since the sacraments are those special acts of Christ in the Church, it is important that those who receive or celebrate the sacraments have a living faith in Christ and be active members of the Church.

In the case of baptism, therefore, it is expected that the parents and godparents of the child to be baptized are members of the Church and in some way express their faith in Christ. If this is lacking, what hope is there that the baptized child will be brought up in the faith and become a follower of Christ? In such a case, baptism could become more of a social ritual than a prayerful and religious act.

It is for this reason that in the 1983 Code of Canon Law it is clearly stated that for baptism to be given there must be a well-founded hope that the infant will be brought up in the Catholic religion. If this hope is *altogether* lacking, then the baptism ought to be put off or postponed according to local laws of the diocese and the parents are to be given reasons for this (canon 868).

Therefore, to answer your question specifically, baptism can be *postponed* when there is strong evidence that the infant will not be raised a Catholic. This postponement, however, should be based on local laws of the diocese and should be seen not as a punishment but as a pastoral opportunity for the parents of the child to examine their relationship with Christ and the Church. In other words, the reason for the postponement is to provide them with the time to deal with deeper issues and perhaps bring about healing and growth in faith. Indeed, a child who is brought up in a family of faith has a much better chance of coming to know and love God and thereby find true happiness.

MICHAEL H. GOSSELIN

4. BAPTISMAL RECORD FOR ADOPTIONS

I was married and divorced and my new husband has adopted my child. My son's name is now legally changed. I called my pastor and asked him to change the child's name in the baptismal register but he says it can't be done because it amounts to tampering with a church document. Is this true?

What your pastor told you is essentially correct. The sacramental registers are to indicate what actually took place with whom, not to reflect what people would rather have them say later on. However, notations regarding adoption, change of name, and so on, are easily and correctly made in a section that is provided in every baptismal register called "notations." Should a notation run into great detail, or should there be a request for some type of special handling of a particular entry, the notation can either be continued in the inside front or back covers of the sacramental register or, better, added in a separate book of notations which is kept in the parish along with the other registers.

Some civil authorities have buckled under to the revisionist tendencies of people who want changes made in their vital information. One case involved a man whose mother and father divorced. The mother subsequently married a much younger man who was only slightly older than the person in question. The new husband legally adopted the fellow, and the birth certificate (even the microfilmed copy) was actually obliterated and changed to show that the new husband was the real father—even though he would have been only a child himself when "his" child was conceived!

It is difficulties like these that the Church tries to avoid in insisting that once a record is made, there are to be no changes on the original document. Even corrections of spelling or date should be recorded in the notations. In the case at hand, an appropriate notation might read: "Adopted by (name of new husband) at (place), (date). All future certificates should list only this name as the father."

DENNIS W. MORROW

5. CONFIRMATION SPONSORS

*Our pastor will not allow my mother to be my sponsor for confirmation.
What does church law say about sponsors for baptism and confirmation?*

Church law stipulates that sponsors at baptism and confirmation
must be persons other than one's parents. The confusion on this point
arises from an interpretation given to a document from Rome which
was issued in August 1971. The document established the new rite of
confirmation as we have it in the Church today. In the wording of this
document it seemed acceptable for parents to act as sponsors for their
children. Although the misunderstanding was cleared up in a supple-
mentary document, the practice was allowed in many localities and
continued until the 1983 Code of Canon Law clearly stated that parents
are not to be sponsors of their own children.

Sponsors date back to ancient custom in the early church where
adults who wished to enter the Christian community through baptism
were asked to have persons from the Christian community vouch for
their integrity and motives. This type of screening was needed in the
hostile situations the Church often found itself.

Through the centuries, sponsorship with the sacraments of baptism
and confirmation took on the character of assistance to parents carrying out their awesome responsibilities of raising their children in the
faith, particularly when infant baptism became ordinary practice in the
Church. Sponsorship is subject to different cultural emphases from
place to place. In some cultures, for example, a sponsor becomes practically a relative and can even take charge of rearing a minor in case of
great illness or death of one's parents.

The sponsor's tasks are grave as the Church envisions them. The
Church sees the task of raising young people in the faith so important
that parents cannot do it, always and everywhere, alone. They need
assistance from another adult(s) in the community who are willing to
commit themselves to the one sponsored with care, faith and example
along the difficult journey of life.

For this reason, for both baptism and confirmation church law expects a sponsor: (1) to be a confirmed Catholic; (2) to be at least sixteen years of age; (3) to be designated by the parents or guardians;

(4) to have indicated willingness to undertake this obligation; and (5) to be leading a life in harmony with the faith.

The code also suggest that one's sponsor at confirmation is most appropriately one's sponsor from baptism. In this way, the important task already accepted by the baptismal sponsor is continued and brought to completion.

The confirmation ritual provides for the possibility of parents presenting their children to the bishop in the ceremony but the long-range task of sponsor and model in the faith is still to be given to another adult.

JOSEPH N. PERRY

6. COMMUNION FAST

Are there rules any more in the Church about fasting before receiving Communion?

In the 1983 Code of Canon Law, canon 919 treats the matter of the Communion fast. It covers three categories of persons and situations. A general prescription is given first; then exceptions to this general prescription are explained

First, anyone planning to receive Communion is to fast from any food or drink for at least one hour before actually receiving. Water and medicine may be taken at any time.

Second, a priest celebrating two or three Masses in one day need observe the fasting law only before the first Mass.

Third, the elderly, the sick, and those who care for them are not bound by the fasting law.

A few observations are in order. The reception of the Eucharist is not a game to be played with a stop watch. The fast is important, but pales in comparison to a devout reception of the sacrament. "Medicine" is not defined in the canon; presumably, vitamins taken at a doctor's recommendation would, for instance, be included. The canon says nothing about alcohol which must consequently fall into the category of food and drink unless it is used for legitimate medicinal purposes.

The sick are those who suffer from some infirmity, not necessarily those confined to bed. A diabetic who must take frequent small meals would belong to this group, for example. Who are the elderly? In the United States, if you are a "senior citizen" for Social Security purposes, you could certainly consider yourself to be exempt from the obligatory Communion fast.

Family members or nurses need not refrain from receiving Communion if they have been eating when the priest or Eurcharistic minister arrives with Communion for the sick. Finally, one who has not been planning to receive Communion but is unexpectly presented with an opportunity to do so ought not to pass it up because a full hour has not elapsed since food or drink was consumed. The priority, as we stated above, lies with the Eucharist; the fast, while important, is secondary.

DENNIS W. MORROW

7. COMMUNION TWICE IN A DAY

I was under the impression that a person can go to Communion only once in a day. Has this rule changed?

In a certain sense, yes. But it needs some explanation.

Under the previous law of the Church, there were two exceptions to the rule that a person could only receive Holy Communion once a day. The first was an exception for those in danger of death (even if they had received Communion earlier in the same day). The second was for the feasts of Christmas and Easter when a person could receive Communion twice.

The 1983 code extends that permission and states: "A person who has received the Most Holy Eucharist may receive it again on the same day only during the celebration of the Eurcharist in which the person participates" (canon 917). The important point here is that receiving Communion is not seen as an isolated action, but as an integral part of the entire celebration of the Eucharist. The liturgy of the Word, the offering of the gifts, the Eucharistic prayer and the reception of Holy Communion combine to form one complete act of worship. So, even though you have already received Holy Communion on a given day, if you participate in a celebration of the Eucharist—a Mass—you may receive again.

It is in this way that the "rules" you asked about have changed. It remains, however, that the reception of Holy Communion more than once a day *apart* from participation in Mass is an exception for those in danger of death.

Edward G. Pfnausch

8. COMMUNION AND NON-CATHOLICS

Someone at work told me that Catholics can receive Communion if they are at a wedding or funeral in a non-Catholic church. Is this true?

In general this is not true. Canon 844, §1 of the Code of Canon Law states that Catholic ministers lawfully administer the sacraments only to Catholics; likewise Catholics lawfully receive sacraments only from Catholic ministers. Since this includes Catholics of any rite, Latin Rite Catholics may receive Communion in Eastern Rite Churches.

Section 2 of canon 844 gives an exception to this general rule. A Catholic may receive the sacraments of penance, Eucharist, and the anointing of the sick in non-Catholic churches under certain conditions. A principal condition is that it must be a church in which these sacraments are recognized as valid by the Catholic Church. All the sacraments of the Eastern non-Catholic Churches, commonly known as the Orthodox, are viewed as valid by the Catholic Church. Some other smaller churches also have seven valid scaraments because, like the Orthodox, they have preserved the substance of the Eucharist, the sacrament of orders, and apostolic succession. By contrast, a Catholic may not receive Communion in a Protestant church or other church lacking one of these essential characteristics, as determined by the Apostolic See.

For a Catholic who would wish to receive Communion in an Orthodox or other church which is recognized as having a valid Eucharist, there must be pressing need for such an action and some spiritual advantage to be gained. For instance, the Catholic party may have been unable to go to his or her own church.

One further condition, though not stated in canon law, is that the Catholic should request permission of the Orthodox or other non-Catholic ministers before receiving in that church. The Orthodox often are not as receptive to sacramental sharing with Catholics as Catholics are with them, so this permission should be obtained as an ecumenical courtesy.

To return to the original question, one should note that very few non-Catholic churches have Communion services at weddings or funerals. The more common occurrence is the non-Catholic Christian who wishes to receive Communion at a Catholic wedding or funeral. The Orthodox and other non-Catholics who are recognized as having a valid Eucharistist are welcome to receive Communion in Roman Catholic churches if they ask on their own for it and they are properly disposed (canon 844, §3).

For a Protestant or other Christian denomination which is not recognized as having a valid Eucharist, the legal question is complicated. Canon law requires a "grave reason" to administer the Eucharist to such Christians, and it is up to the bishop or the episcopal conference to determine cases that constitute grave reason (canon 844, §§4 and 5). Few dioceses explicitly recognize a wedding or funeral as a case of grave necessity. Your parish priest will no doubt be aware of your local diocesan policies concerning a baptized non-Catholic receiving Communion in a Catholic Church.

JOHN M. HUELS, O.S.M.

9. COMMUNION MINISTERS

In my sister's parish only the priests distribute Communion at the weekend Masses but in my parish there are Ministers of the Eucharist. What might be the reason for this difference?

The difference in the practice of ministers of the Eucharist between your home parish and your sister's rests largely in pastoral need and practice. The Code of Canon Law, in canon 910, says that the ordinary ministers of Holy Communion are the bishop, the priest and the deacon. It adds that there are extraordinary ministers (including the installed acolyte) who are deputed to this responsibility. Canon 230, which speaks of extraordinary ministers of the Eucharist, says they may be designated whenever the needs of the Church warrant it, and when ordinary ministers are lacking.

Extraordinary ministers of Holy Communion were one of the subjects mentioned by Pope Paul VI in the instruction *Immensae caritatis*, issued on January 29, 1973. The Pope said such extraordinary ministers may be appointed (1) when no ordinary ministers are available, (2) when ordinary ministers cannot perform their ministry because of illness or old age, and (3) when the large number of the faithful requesting the sacrament would unduly prolong the distribution.

Pope Paul VI also said such extraordinary ministers are to be appointed by the local ordinary (i.e., by diocesan bishops, vicars general or episcopal vicars). They may assist by distributing the Eucharist during the celebration of Mass, and may carry it outside Mass to the infirmed and aged.

Today, in this country and elsewhere, thousands of persons serve as extraordinary ministers of the Eucharist. They assist the priests and deacons in distributing the Eucharist at Mass, and they bring it to the elderly and sick of our parishes. They perform an extremely important service to our Christian communities and reestablish for all of us a vital avenue of lay involvement in the liturgy which was present in the early centuries of the Church.

JOHN A. RENKEN

10. MASS SERVERS

My daughter is getting very angry because her brother can serve Mass in our parish and she cannot. Why does the Church have this rule?

Your daughter has good reason for her question as the reason for the exclusion of girls or women as altar servers is not entirely clear in church law. There is, however, wide possibility for official liturgical functions for both women and men today.

"Altar server" is a traditional function within the Mass derived from the former minor order of acolyte. Today as in the past the Church restricts the *permanent exercise* of this ministry to men who are preparing for sacred ordination as priest or deacon. Current church discipline also makes provision for lay men to be installed as acolytes on a somewhat stable basis if they have the requisite age and formation.

Except for seminaries and religious houses, the position of acolyte has not been widely used. Parishes in the United States have the custom of using altar servers, a function exercised almost exclusively by children, always boys, as women were not permitted in the sanctuary during the offering of the Mass. This prescription against having women in the sanctuary, of course, is not dropped from liturgical discipline. Some parishes today who permit girls or women as altar servers usually proceed with the reasoning that in our culture, altar serving has traditionally been a children's ministry. Also, one opinion sees no clear reasoning for excluding women from altar service when, in fact today, they can function with most other liturgical ministries not reserved to the priest.

The 1983 Code of Canon Law opens to women and men the *temporary exercise* of the office of lector, as well as the ministry of auxiliary distributor of Holy Communion and other such liturgical functions local bishops may establish, provided these persons have the requisite formation and appointment. In certain needy areas designated women and men are allowed by church law to exercise the ministry of the Word, preside over liturgical prayer, confer baptism, and witness marriages. In light of these ministerial rights spoken of clearly in the law it would seem illogical to continue to exclude women from service at the altar.

Nevertheless, on April 3, 1980 an Instruction on Worship issued by the Sacred Congregation for the Doctrine of the Faith and approved by Pope John Paul II stated clearly, among other items, that while other liturgical ministries are open to women they are to be excluded as altar servers. The 1983 Code of Canon Law does not mention this specific issue.

I submit the few distinctions between men and women that remain in church law are not always clear as to their reasoning. The fact remains, in the opinion of this writer, that a good argument can be made for either admitting or excluding women as altar servers based on what still seems to remain from former discipline and tradition and the direction that ministerial development is taking in the Church.

A sound interpretation would point out that while former discipline refused them, current discipline appears, logically, open to women in this regard. I believe one has to have patience with bishops, pastors and pastoral experiences that fall on either side of opinion on this question. Some will apply church discipline strictly; others will apply it creatively.

JOSEPH N. PERRY

11. SUNDAY MASS ON VACATION

We are planning a two week vacation cruise. My wife now says we cannot go because we know beforehand that there will be no Sunday Mass available on board the ship. Is she right?

In the 1983 Code of Canon Law, it is canon 1247 that requires the participation of the faithful in the Mass on all Sundays and other holy days.

In canon 1248, §2, however, we are told that "if because of lack of a sacred minister or for other grave cause participation in the celebration of the Eucharist is impossible, it is specially recommended that the faithful take part in the liturgy of the word if it is celebrated in the parish church or in another sacred place according to the prescriptions of the diocesan bishop, or engage in prayer for an appropriate amount of time personally or in a family or, as occasion offers, in groups of families."

If you are at sea, and no priest is on board to celebrate Mass, it seems that participation in the Eucharist will be impossible. This once in the year (possibly once in a lifetime) voyage would surely be a sufficient "cause" or reason for being in this situation of impossibility to participate in the Eucharist. This presumes you do regularly attend Sunday Mass and you are not going out to sea to escape the obligation.

The code, however, clearly recommends that we do *something* on that day, even if we cannot participate in the Eucharist. You are to spend an "appropriate amount of time" in prayer, at least.

I would *recommend* that you take a missal or bible with the prayers and readings for that Sunday along with you and use it to center your prayer time. That, however, is only a recommendation; canon 1248 leaves the particular selection of prayer to you, although encouraging participation in the liturgy of the word in a parish church or other sacred place.

The bottom line is: Go. Have a good time! Just don't forget to pray.

WILLIAM E. GOLD

12. HOLYDAYS OF OBLIGATION

Is it true that there are fewer holydays of obligation in the 1983 code?

In a word, no. Some confusion had arisen because when the 1983 code was in its final stages of development, it listed the holydays of obligation as Christmas and one feast of the Blessed Mother to be decided by the bishops of each country. That final draft of the code was sent to the Pope for his approval and the changes he made in the text were not known for a few months. Thus, when the code was promulgated in January 1983, many press releases quoted the document sent *to* the Pope, which was different from the document which he eventually approved.

The document sent to the Pope listed two obligation days; the final version of the code lists ten. These are the same days as were listed in the 1917 code: Christmas, Epiphany, Ascension, Corpus Christi, Mary the Mother of God, Immaculate Conception, Assumption, St. Joseph, Sts. Peter and Paul, and All Saints (canon 1246).

The bishops of any country, if a sufficient number of them agree, can abolish any of these obligation days or transfer the celebration of any of the feasts to a Sunday. If no action is taken by the bishops, the Catholic population of the country would be expected to observe all ten days of obligation.

In the late 19th century the bishops of this country reduced the number of obligation days to six: Christmas, Ascension, Mary the Mother of God, Assumption, Immaculate Conception, and All Saints. At their meeting in November 1983, the bishops considered reducing the days to three: Christmas, Immaculate Conception, and All Saints. For a variety of reasons they chose to leave the six days as they have been. It is possible that at some time in the future they will reconsider this question of days of obligation, or may look at the possibility of moving the celebration of some of these great feasts in the Church to an appropriate Sunday, but for now, the Catholic Church in this country has made no changes in this matter.

ROYCE R. THOMAS

13. CONFESSION BEFORE COMMUNION

My mother will not go to Communion unless she has gone to confession the day before. Was this a law in the Church at one time?

The Church has never had a law requiring confession on the day before the reception of Communion. If your mother is a weekly church-goer it is easy to understand how she could fall into such a pattern because in most parishes confessions are held on Saturdays and often on the day before a holy day of obligation. Moreover, the Church's pastors and educators traditionally have urged frequent confession for one's spiritual betterment, even when one has only venial sins or no sins at all to confess.

However, the Church also desires that the faithful should participate fully in the Eucharistic celebration, including partaking of the sacred bread and cup. The inability to confess should not prevent a person from receiving Communion if that person is not in mortal sin and is otherwise eligible to receive.

The law which requires confession before Communion is basically the same today as it has been for centuries. It obliges only those who are conscious, that is, who are *certain* of having committed serious sin to confess before receiving Communion. This teaching of the Church was confirmed at the Council of Trent in 1551 and included in the 1917 Code of Canon Law, and it appears in canon 916 of the 1983 code.

Canon 916 also says that if there is a serious reason for receiving Communion and there is no opportunity to confess, even those in serious sin may receive Communion without first confessing. The gravity of the reason for receiving Communion depends to a great extent on the individual's spiritual needs and motivation. For some persons serious reasons for receiving Communion in such a case might include: the possibility of embarrassment upon not receiving; the importance of the occasion, such as a wedding, funeral, or feast day; sincere spiritual need for the grace of the sacrament; strong desire to participate fully in the Eucharistic celebration.

In all such cases the person in serious sin must make an act of perfect contrition before receiving Communion, either by reciting devoutly and meaningfully a standard act of contrition or expressing to God sorrow for sin in one's own words.

An act of perfect contrition, according to canon 916, also includes the *intention* of confessing one's serious sins as soon as possible. One does not have to fulfill this intention as soon as it is physically possible, but rather as soon as possible without great inconvenience to the penitent or the confessor. It would suffice to confess at the next regularly scheduled time for confessions. If one cannot go to confession at this time or on another regularly scheduled time in subsequent weeks, one should arrange to see a confessor at some other time.

JOHN M. HUELS, O.S.M.

14. FIRST PENANCE AND FIRST COMMUNION

Is it a law that children must receive the sacrament of penance before making their First Communion? One priest in my town says it is a law, but another disagrees.

It is not surprising that the two priests disagree because the law could be easily misunderstood. The Code of Canon Law, canon 914, states in part that it is primarily the duty of parents, and also pastors, to see that children who have reached the use of reason are prepared properly for their First Communion and receive it as early as possible, preceded by sacramental confession. The law presumes that a child attains the use of reason by age seven.

This canon is directed not to children but to parents and pastors. Since it is their duty to prepare children for First Communion, it is also their responsibility to prepare them for first penance so that the sacrament is truly available for those children who need or desire it.

According to church doctrine defined at the Council of Trent and affirmed in canons 916, 960, and 988, only those in serious (mortal) sin must go to confession before receiving Communion. Therefore if a child has committed a serious sin, sacramental confession must precede reception of Communion.

Some experts maintain that a young child is developmentally incapable of committing serious sin. Nevertheless, the law recommends that the faithful also confess their venial sins (canon 988, §2), but this is not obligatory.

Like all Catholics, children have the right to receive the Eucharist if they are properly disposed and have the use of reason. Such children may not be refused the sacrament, even if they do not make their confession first (canons 213, 843).

In practice, the requirement of the use of reason is not strictly enforced in the case of developmentally disabled persons, such as the mentally handicapped. They are prepared for the sacraments in special programs regulated by diocesan law.

JOHN M. HUELS, O.S.M.

15. PENANCE SERVICES

I live on the border of two dioceses. In one, the parishes often have communal penance services, and in the other they are not permitted. Are such services "legal"? Why do these dioceses differ in this practice?

In attempting to answer this question I am very much aware that any effort is beset on all sides with the possibility of misunderstanding. To avoid such misunderstanding I might restructure the inquiry by making a distinction between communal penance services during which there are individual confessions heard, and communal penance services where general absolution is given with no individual confessions being heard. It is usually in this second circumstance that questions such as yours arise.

Canon 960 in the 1983 Code of Canon Law states very clearly that individual and integral confession is "the ordinary" or usual way for persons to be reconciled with God and the Church. A communal penance service during which individual confessions are heard is clearly operating within this "ordinary" form of reconciliation. For a parish to have such a service or not is a matter of liturgical preference. However, the same canon indicates that physical or moral impossibility may excuse a person from individual confession, in which case reconciliation may take place in another way.

Canon 961 takes up the matter of general absolution and indicates those exceptional circumstances within which this form of reconciliation may not only be permitted, but even called for. One of these instances, described in the canon as "serious necessity," arises when a large number of penitents gather for the sacrament and there are not sufficient priests available to hear individual confessions within a reasonable time, thereby depriving the faithful of the grace of the sacrament of penance or the sacrament of the Eucharist for an extended period of time through no fault of their own. The canon goes on to stipulate that it is not to be considered sufficient necessity if confessors cannot be readily available because of the great number of penitents on the occasion of a "great feast or pilgrimage" (canon 961, §2). In other words, the problem cannot be a temporary one.

In the final section of canon 961 it is left to the diocesan bishop to judge whether conditions required for general absolution are present in a given situation. In most dioceses bishops have issued guidelines which establish those conditions under which they will allow general absolution.

The problem presented in the original question probably arises from the fact that in one diocese a bishop sees the requirements as being fulfilled and thus allows general absolution at reconciliation services, while in the adjoining diocese another bishop does not see the requirements fulfilled there. Thus, in this second diocese reconciliation services where general absolution would be imparted are not permitted.

Basically, the law allows for different options. Dioceses differ in practice because circumstances differ and because bishops are different as well.

DALE CALHOUN

16. HEALING SERVICE

We recently had a "Healing Service" at our parish. Is this type of thing common in the Catholic Church? Are people able to heal and cure as Jesus did?

The expression "healing service" can mean many things. Usually, there is a service in which healing is prayed for and God is free to grant it or not, fully or partially, now or later. It is intercessory prayer which anyone may make and thus is not automatic or magical.

Sometimes, the healing prayers occur during the intercessory prayers of a prayer group meeting. On other occasions a group may come together for the express purpose of praying for healing. One faith healer says she leads praise services and is given the knowledge someone is healed.

Since Christ left his gift of healing with the Church it is a part of the mission of the Church. It is usually exercised in the context of evangelization and forgiveness and looks to healing the whole person. Many times healing affects and is affected by resentments, pride, selfishness, etc.

Some individuals may also participate in this mission of healing, as St. Paul wrote: "In the Church, God has put all in place: in the first place apostles, in the second place prophets, and in the third place teachers; then those who perform miracles, followed by those who are given the power to heal or to help others . . ." (1 Cor. 12:28). Nowadays, these healing services almost always recognize the ecclesial dimension and take place in connection with the sacraments, especially Eucharist, penance and anointing of the sick.

Just about every diocese has an office or liaison with the charismatic renewal. For more information you could contact them.

ROYCE R. THOMAS

17. ANOINTING THE SICK

Why has the sacrament of "Extreme Unction" been given a new name?
Are the last rites given to people after they have died?

The Second Vatican Council suggested that anointing of the sick is a more appropriate name for the sacrament than extreme unction, which means "last anointing." In the early Church the practice of anointing the sick with oil was not limited to those near death, as seen in the Epistle of James 5:14-15. However, in the Middle Ages deathbed anointing increasingly became the practice, though the Church never lost sight of the original purpose of anointing. The 16th century Council of Trent decreed that one of the effects of the sacrament is physical health when this is expedient for the soul.

Since a potential effect of the sacrament is the restoration of health, it is improper to limit its celebration to those who are in danger of death. It is also incorrect to refer to the anointing as the "last rites." The last sacrament of the Church is Viaticum—Holy Communion given to the dying. If possible the anointing should be given before a person reaches the moment of death.

Who may be anointed? According to canon law, those who are *seriously* ill, namely, those who begin to be in danger due to illness or old age. This includes those who are to undergo surgery for a serious illness, elderly persons who are in a notably weakened condition, and seriously ill children who have sufficient use of reason to be strengthened by the sacrament.

No sacrament may *ever* be given to a dead person. This is a serious abuse. However, the sacrament may be given if there is a doubt whether the person is dead. Also the sacrament may be given to children if there is a doubt whether they have the use of reason. It may be given to persons who are unconscious if they would have at least implicitly asked for it when they were in control of their faculties.

It is an abuse of the sacrament to administer it indiscriminately. Anointing of the sick is not intended for minor illnesses or routine surgery, but is a special rite of the Church for its seriously ill members.

JOHN M. HUELS, O.S.M.

25

18. BURIAL FROM CHURCH

When my sister died several years ago, we were not allowed to bury her from Church. Our pastor said it was because she was divorced and remarried. My husband's marriage to me is his second one. Will I have to face the same situation if he dies before me?

No, you won't. The laws concerning Christian burial in the Church have changed a great deal in recent times.

Under the old law, Christian burial was to be denied to anyone who was excommunicated by the Church. This included people who were divorced and remarried without permission of a church court. The denial of Christian burial to excommunicated people was seen in the old days to be a combination of penance for breaking the law of Christ and a deterrant to those who might be contemplating such a step.

With Vatican II, the philosophy of the Church changed. Penalties, excommunications and censures were cut to a bare minimum because the essence of the teaching of Jesus was seen as love, not punishment. Specifically, people who enter a second marriage without church clearance still have a problem of their sacramental rights in the Christian community, but they are not excommunicated.

Also, the new law emphasizes the fact that no one should be denied Christian burial except for the most serious of causes, e.g., those who have given up the faith publicly or those whose openly sinful lives would cause great public scandal.

The reason for this change of heart is clear. Christian burial is really for the sake of the survivors, and cannot touch the deceased as any kind of penalty. Jesus preached and practiced a wonderful forgiveness and mercy towards sinners. The Church, if it is to be true to the Lord, can do no less.

THOMAS J. LYNCH

19. CREMATION FOR CATHOLICS

Is it now permissible for Catholics to be cremated? When did this rule change?

Cremation of the bodily remains of the deceased has been an acceptable option for Latin Rite Catholics since 1963.

In the past the Church reacted to certain individuals and groups who chose cremation of the body as a public protest against Christian belief in the resurrection of the body. Such anti-Christian sentiment is no longer apparent in these times.

The earliest tradition of the Church shows us that Christians began burying the bodies of their dead much akin to the ancient Jews. The catacombs and bodily relics of the saints and martyrs give evidence of the dignified burial rites of the early Christians even though cremation was a usual practice in ancient pagan Rome.

Under the Holy Roman Emperors cremation all but disappeared. In fact, there was no reason for the Church's public disapproval of cremation until an upsurge in the practice occurred across Christian Europe in the 19th century. Then, in reaction, the Holy See in 1886 forbade Catholics to cremate the bodies of those who died. To further emphasize the Church's intolerance of the practice the first codification of church law (1917) stipulated that those whose bodies were to be cremated would be denied funeral rites in the Church (1917 code, canon 1240, §5).

In modern times it has become evident that a number of countries no longer proportion land for cemeteries and tombs. Cremation is, in fact, a necessity in certain parts of the world for clear hygienic and economic reasons.

In the 1983 Code of Canon Law the Church now presumes that one's choice of cremation has nothing to do with denial of faith unless the contrary is evident (canon 1184). Thus, it is an acceptable practice for Catholics.

Presently, in the funeral rite there exists no provision for bringing the ashes to the church. The Church's final rites are designed to pay honor to the bodily remains with the use of symbols such as holy water, white shroud, incense, candles etc. With the choice to cremate, nevertheless, the funeral Mass is usually celebrated separate from the interment of the ashes.

JOSEPH N. PERRY

20. DONATING BODY FOR MEDICAL RESEARCH

What is the Church's position on donating one's body to science for medical research? What if there is no burial?

In recent years there has been an increasing practice of listing one's self as an organ donor, or even of providing for the donation of one's body for scientific research after death. The Church's law does not prohibit this, but common Catholic teaching would require at least some safeguards.

First, Catholics believe in the resurrection of the body. Respect for the body of a dead person is an ancient dimension of Catholic belief and practice: this body was the temple of the Holy Spirit, and one day will rise to eternal glory. It must be treated as more than a carcass, and is due appropriate respect by all concerned. So, the donation of one's body must be done is such a way that true respect is expressed for the body and the Church's teaching on resurrection is not denied.

Second, the donation must be expressed in a way that the person's will is truly known. An ancient principle of church law is that the will of the donor, including the donor of one's body, must be respected. But to respect it, that will must be known. In many states this is taken care of by the donor's card which can be filled out and registered when a driver's license is obtained. The same expression of will can be done in a "Last Will and Testament."

Third, after the organ transplant or scientific medical research has been completed, the remains of the body must be fittingly disposed of. This can be done through cremation, or by burial. The laws of many states require this, and most medical research facilities safeguard this practice through their own internal norms.

The revised funeral rites of the Church provide for the celebration of a Mass of the Resurrection without the body present. When the body has been donated for medical research, it may be some time before the research involved has been completed. In such a circumstance, it would be fitting to hold the celebration of the Mass of the Resurrection without the body present. Burial, or the proper disposition of the ashes if cremation is used, would take place later in a fitting manner, usually in a private ceremony.

JAMES H. PROVOST

21. MARRIAGE POLICY

In my diocese there is a policy that marriage dates, etc., must be arranged with the parish priest at least six months in advance. Is this required in all dioceses and under what circumstances could exceptions be made?

NOTICE

Couples wishing to marry must notify one of the priests at least six (6) months in advance.

Many parishes across the country have similar notices directed to any Catholic couple planning to receive the sacrament of matrimony. This is done because many dioceses have devised a pastoral policy for marriage preparation. Canon 1063 of the Code of Canon Law obliges pastors to see to it that their people are properly prepared for marriage, "so that the matrimonial state is maintained in a Christian spirit and makes progress toward perfection." It is for this reason, the building of Christian marriages characterized by faith, love and maturity, that marriage preparation policies have been adopted by many dioceses.

Christian marriage involves a life long process of growth and faithful commitment to a continuing, supportive relationship in which each partner helps the other to develop as fully as possible. A serious concern for pre-marriage preparation must consist of both spiritual and human enrichment. This takes *time*; hence, the reason for a policy of marriage preparation of some six months or more. The Church believes that unless it speaks positively of marriage by exposing and highlighting the ideals and qualities of Christian marriage, the present rate of separation and divorce among Catholics will continue to accelerate. The Church in many dioceses recognizes the need to assist engaged couples to find for themselves a Christian lifestyle which takes marriage seriously.

At a time in the life of the Church when careful preparation is made for reception of the Sacraments of Eucharist, penance and confirmation and in many places there are pre-baptism programs for young parents, preparation for marriage should not be limited to merely determining the absence of church law impediments. Again, *time* is needed to help a couple explore the emotional, personal, social and spiritual dimensions of Christian marriage, and therefore a period of some months for marriage preparation is needed.

There is, however, an exception to every rule. There are circumstances which *could* shorten or abbreviate the procedures for marriage preparation, but these vary from diocese to diocese. Generally, older people seeking to marry might have the preparation time adjusted, but the best source of information on this point will be your parish staff or the personnel in your diocesan chancery or marriage tribunal.

BRIAN R. CORMIER

22. PARISH FOR MARRIAGE

What are the rules in canon law about what parish people can be married in?

Canon law does set forth norms for the celebration of marriage as to place and proper officiant. Marriages where at least one of the parties is a Latin Rite Catholic must take place in the parish church before one's pastor. It is generally assumed in the law that a Catholic has a pastor and the parish church where one's pastor or parish priest is assigned is the church where one's marriage would normally be celebrated. Only by exception would a wedding be celebrated in some other church or oratory, and then with the pastor's permission. Consequently, when a couple plans to marry, initial contact is made with the pastor of one of the proposed spouses.

Custom suggests that the wedding be celebrated in the Church of the bride, but for the valid celebration of the marriage, the pastor of either may officiate. If the pastor of the church does not officiate, then a priest or deacon properly delegated by the pastor will do so.

The purpose of the law here is not to complicate the details and options involved in planning a wedding, but simply to maintain order concerning the sacrament of matrimony and to allow for record keeping.

Also, just as in civil law, officials with the faculties to witness marriages for the state can do so only within their circumscribed jurisdictions. In the Church a bishop or priest can witness marriages in the name of the Church only within the limits of his territory. For a bishop, this will mean anywhere in his diocese. For a pastor or parish priest or deacon it will mean the territorial confines of the parish to which he is assigned and when at least one of the parties in the marriage is subject to his pastoral care.

To witness a marriage outside his territory *validly*, a parish priest or deacon would need delegation—authorization—from the bishop or pastor of the place where the wedding is to be celebrated.

In marriages where the parties are of different faiths the wedding can be celebrated in the non-Catholic church provided permission has been obtained by the Catholic party from the bishop or person in the diocese competent to grant that permission. The necessary promises must be made by the Catholic party. The parish priest usually assists in making these arrangements and handles the paper work involved.

JOSEPH N. PERRY

23. MARRIAGE OUTSIDE PARISH CHURCH BUILDING

My fiancé and I, both Catholic, want to be married by a priest, but in a nearby Presbyterian church because of the location of the building and its very beautiful interior. Is this permissible?

We're sorry that so many of these answers must seem evasive or highly qualified: but the response to your question must be, "Yes, and no." Or more accurately, "Permissible, but not probable."

Let me explain the reasoning. It has always been the conviction of the Roman Catholic worshipping community that your marriage is something out of the ordinary. It is your day in a very special way: a day for public proclamation to all that the two of you are marrying, as we really believe, "in the Lord."

Therefore your marriage is at the Eucharist, and in the public gathering of the local church—in its place of worship, with your presiding priest or deacon, and your official public witnesses who are also those closest to you.

Occasionally, the ceremony itself might be permitted in some place other than "a sacred place," other therefore than in a church, perhaps in the garden, or in the living room, or on a mountaintop. Supervision of this, and individual approval of requests, comes from the local guide of the worshipping community, its bishop. The danger is that the requests might get frivolous; thus, each request and the reasons for it must be weighed carefully.

This is in keeping with the 1983 Code of Canon Law (canon 1118) which states that the parish church is the proper place for two Catholics to be married, but that the local ordinary may permit the marriage to be celebrated "in some other suitable place." It is implied that such a permission would be given if there was a good reason for the request. However, it is up to each local ordinary to decide what constitutes a "good reason" in his diocese. You must consult with your parish and diocesan representatives and see if your reasons, location and beautiful interior of the church, are weighty enough for the permission to be given.

Every locality has its particular flavor and style. So the answer to your question has to be that it is theoretically possible and permissible but perhaps not completely the way of best celebrating your commitment to each other in the sacrament of matrimony. I suspect that the bishop would urge the celebration of your marriage in its own home, the place where you worship God most solemnly—in your church.

ELLSWORTH KNEAL

24. MIXED MARRIAGE PROMISES

What are the promises about children that must be made before the marriage of a Catholic to a non-Catholic?

Canon 1125 requires that "the Catholic make a sincere promise to do all in his or her power to have all the children baptized and brought up in the Catholic Church." Several points in the canon deserve comment.

First of all it is only the *Catholic* party who makes the promise before the Catholic Church. Non-Catholics are not required to make a promise to the Catholic Church. They might make a private promise to themselves about the religious rearing of the children. Or they might make such a promise to members of their own family or perhaps even to their own church, but they are not required to make such a promise to the Catholic Church.

In requiring only the Catholic party to make a promise to the Catholic Church, there is an implicit recognition that the other party, often a devout member of another Christian Church, might have very strong, conscientious convictions about the religious rearing of the children. The Catholic Church wishes to respect those convictions.

This brings us to a *second* point. The promise made by the Catholic is *not* to have all the children baptized and brought up in the Catholic Church *but to do all in his or her power* to have all the children baptized and brought up in the Catholic Church. The canon means exactly what it says and only what it says. No more.

It envisions, for example, the following case. A devout Lutheran woman and a devout Catholic man wish to marry. Both have convictions about the religious rearing of the children. The Catholic Church expects the man "to do all in his power," i.e., all that is *reasonably* possible to insure the Catholic rearing of the children. It would not be reasonable to expect the man to violate the woman's conscience or to jeopardize the relationship of love and trust between them. It is expected, therefore, that they will work out a compromise that will enable the man "to do all in his power" to see to the Catholic rearing of the children.

The canon, however, also envisions this case. A devout Lutheran woman wishes to marry a nominally Catholic man who has absolutely no interest in the Catholic rearing of the children. Such a man could hardly make the required promise in good faith, and the local bishop, therefore, would not be empowered to permit the marriage.

A *third* point is this. The canon does not require that the promise be made in writing but only that it be made. Some people feel offended by a requirement of a *signed* promise, as though their word were not good enough. The canon regards an oral promise as sufficient.

Finally, here is a *fourth* point. The religious rearing of children is too important and delicate a matter to be swept under the rug until after the marriage, when it could be a major source of dissension between the couple. It is one of the many questions that should be faced before the marriage, faced squarely and sensitively and with respect for each other's faith.

LAWRENCE G. WRENN

25. MARRIAGE DISPENSATION

I am a Catholic. The man I plan to marry has no religion and he has never been baptized. Our parish priest said we need a "dispensation" to marry. What is that and why is it needed?

Let's start out with the general definition of dispensation in church law. It is a relaxation of a merely church law in a particular case. In other words, laws are supposed to be kept by all of us for the common good. However, occasionally circumstances arise which would make it an unneeded or unjustifiable burden for the law to be honored in an individual case. That's when church authority says: I dispense you. You don't have to keep this law at this time.

The Church has had for the last few hundred years a general prohibition in its laws against Catholics marrying non-Catholics, whether baptized or not. This law seems to spring from the conviction of the Church that a unity of faith between spouses is, if not essential, at least crucial to the growth in faith of those in the marriage. In general and as an abstract principle, the Church saw an objective danger to the faith life of its people when those they married did not share the basic truths of the Catholic faith.

But when we move from the general and abstract principle to the particular and concrete case of two specific persons, the picture is often different. For example, when the couple to be married have discussed the differences in their religious backgrounds and have reached mutual agreement on such things as their understanding of marriage, how religion will be practiced in their home, and the religious upbringing of children, then it is easy to see that continuing to prohibit the marriage would be unfair and contrary to the natural right of the people to marry. When such a situation as this arises, as it has in your own situation, the priest or deacon obtains on your behalf a "dispensation" for your mixed marriage to the unbaptized non-Catholic. In a case where the non-Catholic party was validly baptized, it is now a "permission" rather than a dispensation which is sought. Practically speaking, they amount to the same thing. In each situation the intention of the Church is to ensure that your life as a married person is going to be a source of strength and growth for your own faith and that of the community of believers which we call the Church.

THOMAS J. LYNCH

26. MARRIAGE BY NON-CATHOLIC MINISTER

My son is marrying a non-Catholic girl whose father is a minister. Our parish priest said that the wedding can take place at the minister's church and that the minister can officiate. Don't Catholics have to be married by priests?

Basically, yes. But the situation you present in your question needs a little more explanation.

When you married, you probably recall that there was never any question of your being married by anyone other than your own parish priest. You probably learned, and the 1983 Code of Canon Law still requires for all Catholics, that in order to be married "in the Church" it was necessary that you be married by a Catholic priest.

But there has been an important change in this law, and it is widely held that the change is a compassionate and good one. In exactly the case you describe, a Catholic who wishes to marry someone of another faith, a special permission or dispensation can be granted to the Catholic to allow him to be truly and sacramentally married by a minister of another church.

Imagine the feelings of your future daughter-in-law who may have always hoped that at what would be one of the central moments of her life and her religious upbringing, the one who would officiate at her wedding would be her own father, and that the ceremony would take place in her own church where she had prayed so often. Would you not have wished that for yourself?

Such a circumstance is one of the reasons that since 1966 the Catholic Church has permitted dispensations for Catholics who wanted to be married before the minister of their non-Catholic spouse. For the Catholic, that dispensation is needed for the validity of the marriage. It is granted at the Catholic's request, by that person's bishop, and for a sufficiently persuasive reason. The circumstance you mention is considered one of the strongest.

I personally met another situation in which a devout Lutheran family had actually endowed and given a handsome chapel to a small college. The family prayed there and the daughter of the family always hoped to be married there. She asked this of her Catholic fiancé and he, being an

41

equally devout Roman Catholic—and informed—asked for and received this special permission. So don't feel that your son is repudiating his Church and the religious faith in which you brought him up so carefully. He is in fact following it correctly and advantageously.

One other point: interfaith marriages are not uncommon and the frequent custom is to have both religious representatives present and actively participating in the ceremony. Most clergy welcome this arrangement and are most cooperative each with the other.

So pray for your devout daughter-in-law and for your generous son. And enjoy the wedding. It will be as meaningful for them as yours was for you.

ELLSWORTH KNEAL

27. ATTENDANT AT MARRIAGE
OUTSIDE THE CHURCH

May a Catholic be in the wedding party of a non-Catholic friend?
What about being in the wedding party of a Catholic who is marrying
outside the Church?

The response to your first question is clear. Canon 1108 of the Code
of Canon Law requires the presence of two witnesses as part of the
form of the marriage celebration. These witnesses are traditionally the
bridesmaid and the bestman. There are no requirements to be fulfilled
by those who take on these positions, other than being present at the
ceremony and aware that it is taking place; therefore, at a wedding in a
Catholic Church a non-Catholic may certainly be in the wedding party.
Likewise, Catholics can be witnesses at the weddings of non-Catholics.

The second situation you ask about is not explicitly treated in canon
law. I am interpreting "outside the Church" to mean that either the
bride or the groom is Catholic, but because of some circumstance, a
previous marriage for instance, a choice has been made to have a
minister or civil official conduct the wedding ceremony. With no dispensations or permissions obtained, such a ceremony is considered by
the Catholic Church to be invalid. A Catholic, by acting as an official
witness to an invalid ceremony, could be seen as separating himself or
herself from the teachings of the Church concerning the sacrament of
marriage, and in a certain sense, actually standing in opposition to
the Church.

Although, as stated earlier, such a situation is not explicitly mentioned in the code, its inappropriateness can be clearly inferred from a
number of canons. For example: "The Christian faithful are bound by
an obligation, even in their own patterns of activity, to maintain communion with the Church" (canon 209). "In virtue of their baptism and
confirmation lay members of the Christian faithful are witnesses to the
gospel message by word and by the example of a Christian life" (canon
759). Or again, the Christian faithful are to take care to avoid whatever
is not in harmony with the teachings of the Church (see canon 752).
Considering these canons in light of the Church's teaching on marriage,
it would certainly be difficult, if not impossible, to justify the participa-

tion of a Catholic as an official witness at a wedding ceremony seen by the Church as invalid.

It is valuable to point out here that in seeking an answer to your second question, we found in the Code of Canon Law not a clear and direct ruling, but a general principle regarding the behavior and example expected of a member of the Church. From that principle an answer is drawn for a specific situation. Codified law, by its very nature, is meant to be used in this manner.

ELISSA RINERE, C.P.

28. MARRIAGE OF NON-PRACTICING CATHOLICS

Is a Catholic marriage ceremony invalid if the bride and groom have not practiced their religion for years and have no intention of practicing it after the wedding?

Sometimes couples who do not practice their Catholic faith approach the Church in order to get married. Some of these couples no longer even believe in the Church. They want a church wedding for various reasons: to please their parents, to have a "pretty" ceremony, to do what their friends did, etc.

This problem is serious enough that the International Theological Commission addressed it in 1978. The Commission said: "The personal faith of the contracting parties does not constitute the sacramentality of matrimony, but the absence of personal faith compromises the validity of the sacrament." In other words, it is difficult to see how marriages contracted in total lack of faith can be valid sacramental marriages.

This problem is far from being solved. Not even the 1983 Code of Canon Law solves it. Church law flows from the Church's theology and experience and our theology and experience have not yet given us a definitive answer to this problem. Thus, from the narrow perspective of the *legal* validity of marriage, the Church judges that such marriages are presumed to be valid.

However, much more needs to be said. One of the major emphases of the 1983 code is the need for sacramental preparation. There is a new canon (and a long one at that!) that outlines the responsibility of the whole Christian community to prepare young couples for marriage. In this question, therefore, the issue does not seem so much to be the validity of the union, but rather what the Church can do to call a couple back to faith so that their marriage can be seen clearly as a sacramental union.

Today such a couple would probably encounter some difficulty in arranging a marriage in the Church. The priest or deacon working with the couple would probably work with them in a formal marriage preparation program. Moreover, the couple would be expected to show at least some minimal sign of re-establishing their relationship with the Church. Until the couple is adequately prepared and disposed for Christian marriage by beginning again in some way to practice their faith, the priest or deacon might consider the pros and cons of postponing the marriage. This time of marriage preparation is a real opportunity for evangelization and the Church is taking advantage of it for the benefit both of the couple and of the Christian community.

JOHN G. PROCTOR, JR.

29. CONVALIDATING A MARRIAGE

My son and his wife were married by a Justice of the Peace because neither one attended any church. Now they want to return to Church. What do they do about their marriage?

Your son, I presume, is a baptized Catholic. Catholics are required to marry in the presence of a properly authorized assitant, usually the clergy of their parish, and two witnesses. If they fail to do so and marry before someone else (as in your case, a Justice of the Peace), the Church does not consider the marriage to be a canonically valid marriage.

In order to return to the full practice of the Faith, it will be necessary to have the marriage convalidated in the Church. There are two ways to do this.

The usual way is for the couple to marry in the Church. They should see their pastor and discuss their situation with him. He will assist them in evaluating their present relationship, and will prepare them for a marriage in the Church. Church law considers this contracting marriage anew, not merely renewing consent or having the existing marriage "blessed" by the priest.

An alternative manner to have their marriage recognized in the Church is for the priest to obtain a radical sanation for them. "Radical sanation" means the marriage is "healed" from its root or start, so far as the Church is concerned. This is a process whereby the Church will accept the consent they exchanged when they married before the Justice of the Peace provided it continues on both their parts. It must be clear the two of them intend to remain together, and there must be a serious reason to take this alternative. Their pastor will need to obtain this from the bishop. There is no special ceremony required, and no new marrying in the Church has to take place.

JAMES H. PROVOST

30. REMARRIAGE AFTER DIVORCE

My cousin has been married and divorced three times. Now she is making arrangements to be married again, but this time in the Church, and was told that her previous marriages are "no problem." What does this mean?

From the statements about your cousin, I would presume that she is a member of the Catholic Church, and that she has not "abandoned" her faith by becoming a member of a non-Catholic Church. Based on that presumption, let me clarify the "no problem" answer which she was given concerning her three previous unions.

Members of the Catholic Church who wish to enter into marriage are bound to observe the "form" or "manner" of celebration prescribed by the law of the Catholic Church. This "canonical form" is required for the validity of a Catholic marriage, unless a dispensation from it has been granted in special circumstances. This "form" involves the celebration of the marriage before: (1) the pastor of the parish within which the marriage is taking place, or a priest or deacon delegated by him; and (2) two witnesses. People generally refer to these celebrations as "marriage in the (Catholic) Church."

If your cousin did not follow the "canonical form" described above in the celebration of all of her three previous marriages, and she did not receive a dispensation to be married without the "canonical form" of marriage, all her previous unions are considered to be invalid in the eyes of the Catholic Church. To that degree, they are not obstacles for her to marry in the Catholic Church.

However, before she is officially considered to be "free to marry," declarations from the Church concerning the invalidity of each of her previous unions must be obtained from the tribunal of the diocese in which she resides. The priest taking care of the arrangements for her proposed marriage can assist her in obtaining the needed declarations.

Furthermore, in normal circumstances, the new law of the Church adds a new requirement which must be fulfilled before the celebration of her proposed marriage. If your cousin is bound to any of her previous spouses (and/or children) by any natural obligations (for example, financial support), the same priest will need to obtain from the chancery or tribunal of the diocese in which the proposed marriage is to be celebrated, a special permission in order to proceed with the ceremony.

As you can see, although strictly speaking your cousin's three previous marriages probably present "no problem" to her being married in the Catholic Church, the new law of the Church manifests a special sensitivity in its pastoral concern towards spouses and children of previous unions.

OTTO L. GARCIA

31. APPLYING FOR AN ANNULMENT

How do I go about applying for an annulment. What is involved in the process?

The very first thing that I would recommend that you do is to reflect prayerfully on your former marriage and decide whether you truly had a sacramental marriage or not. This is an important first step. If after this prayerful consideration, you believe your marriage should be annuled, then you have several paths you can follow. For most persons, the obvious first step is to see the parish priest. However, he is not the only person who can be of help. Sometimes, the pastoral associate (who may be a woman) can be of assistance, sometimes a friend, sometimes a member of the marriage tribunal itself. Some parishes have a person hired to help parishioners with preparing their marriage cases. The important thing is to make a contact which will result in your receiving preliminary papers to fill in.

The preliminary questionnaire or document varies with the diocese but its essential purpose is to determine if there are grounds for the pursuing of an annulment. If it is judged that there are possible grounds, then you will either be given a longer questionnaire to fill in or be called in for a personal interview. You will also be asked to give the names of two or three persons who can serve as witnesses and give information concerning you and your former marriage. Sometimes the questions will seem highly personal but remember, without concrete facts, the court cannot make a decision. Each "case" is unique and while there are general grounds, the facts substantiating these are individual and personal.

After all the information is gathered, the chief judge assigns a court to study it. This court is made up of an advocate who has your interests at heart and whose job it is to try to prove the nullity of your marriage, a defender of the bond who makes sure that the bonds of marriage are not lightly set aside and that the rights and interests of your former spouse are respected, and the judge(s) who take all the information and make the final decision. This decision is then reviewed by an appelate court.

The length of the process depends upon the circumstances of the marriage, the cooperation of witnesses, your cooperation, and the workload of the tribunal. Declaring the nullity of a marriage bond is not a light matter and the Church has always treated it with great care. However, the process can be a very healing one for the persons concerned. The serious reflection demanded by the process often results in a healing of the many painful memories of the past and helps to pave the way for a more fruitful second union.

MARY WALDEN, O.S.U.

32. ANNULMENTS UNDER THE NEW CODE

I have heard that annulments will be much harder to get now that there is a new Code of Canon Law. Is this true?

This sort of statement, widely expressed these days, cannot be accurately answered in terms of "true" or "false." Since a comparison is being implied in the above statement, it is important to know from which point the comparison is being made.

In the United States, a special set of approved guidelines (called the American Procedural Norms) directed the annulment process after July 1, 1970. These norms ceased to be operative once the 1983 Code of Canon Law went into effect on November 17, 1983. In comparison with the American Procedural Norms, the annulment process is somewhat longer, but not necessarily harder. On the other hand, in comparison with the 1917 Code of Canon Law, the annulment process is less complicated and more up to date.

For instance, in the 1983 Code the grounds for annulment have been expanded reflecting developments which have taken place in church courts in the past 20 years. However, every affirmative decision reached by a court must be either reviewed or reheard by a second court. Only when this mandatory review or appeal results in a second affirmative decision will the annulment be granted.

Whether annulments will be much harder to get under the 1983 code depends in great part on preparations made in each diocese to handle the added work of the appeal. The 1983 code provides the norms to insure that the annulment process will be executed justly and that the decision will be based on authentic church teaching and church law.

Moreover, the 1983 code contains an entire section of norms devoted to the preparation and pastoral care of those desiring to enter marriage. The ultimate goal is to insure that people entering marriage are adequately prepared and sufficiently capable at all levels to celebrate and live out the sacrament of matrimony. Such sound preparation may decrease and ideally eliminate the need for an annulment process.

PAUL S. LOVERDE

33. ANNULMENTS AND LEGITIMACY OF CHILDREN

If an annulment is a statement that a marriage never existed, how can the children from an annulled marriage be anything but illegitimate?

Terms like "annulment" must be used carefully. Civil marriage annulment asks a judge to "say it isn't so." And the judge, if law allows, does so. It really was so, but the judge says no. So, the Church does not grant "annulments," but "declarations of nullity." Is this a word game? No. Annulment means what was a marriage has no effect. A declaration of nullity says what looked like a marriage never, ever was one.

"Legitimate" means "lawful." For children it means "born of lawful wedlock." For a definition of legitimate, then, we must look at the appropriate legal system since legitimacy is defined by law. In the Church it is defined by canon law.

In the 1983 code, canon 1137 states: "Children conceived or born of a valid or putative marriage are legitimate." A putative marriage, according to canon 1061, is one which is not valid but is entered into in good faith by at least one of the parties.

In most marriages declared null by a marriage tribunal today, both parties were in good faith when they wed. The Church says the children are legitimate—"lawful"—because everyone wanted to do right. The defect that caused the invalidity was then undetected, so no ill effect should touch the children. Even where one party knew, but the other did not, that the marriage could not be valid, the children are still "lawful" since at least the party unaware of the defect wanted what was right. Not unless *both* parties were certain of the nullity of their marriage at its beginning would children be "unlawful"—illegitimate.

Many hoped the 1983 code would omit the concepts of legitimacy and illegitimacy; they are of diminishing import in modern law, including modern canon law, and of little practical value.

Those raising this question of legitimacy of children when the Church examines nullity petitions often do so out of hurt and anger over what they think is being done. But tribunals never "declare a winner," establishing one party's guilt and the other's innocence. Tribunals try to answer this question: is it proved that what seemed to be a marriage was—usually through no one's sin or crime—in fact only an attempted marriage? If the answer is "yes," it is a sad fact and it has some consequences, but children's illegitimacy is not one of them.

THOMAS G. DORAN

34. ANNULMENT: WHO DECIDES?

On a marriage tribunal, who actually makes the decision that a marriage is invalid?

After a marriage case has been heard, it is settled by a judge who must be morally certain that the marriage is invalid. The judge summarizes the case by way of argumentation. This summary is called the sentence and contains the judgment that the marriage is invalid.

The present Code of Canon Law states that there may be either a "college" of three judges who hear a marriage case or a single judge. Only clerics—priests or deacons—can be single judges on a tribunal. After hearing all the evidence, that single judge comes to a decision and writes the sentence. If there is a team of three judges, one of these three may be a layperson, but the other two must be clerics. In this "collegiate" setting a majority vote is required for the marriage to be declared invalid.

As stated above, the judge must reach moral certainty in deciding the invalidity of the marriage. This is a crucial concept in nullity procedures. What does it mean that moral certainty is necessary for the judge to make a decision? An easy way to answer that question is to describe what moral certainty is *not*. It is not absolute certainty, but neither is it only probability. Much has been written by canon lawyers concerning this concept of "moral certainty" and it is the task of each tribunal judge to understand the concept, to weigh the facts of each case carefully, and to reach a decision which takes these factors into consideration in the light of church law.

Each decision issued by a judge is automatically appealed to a second tribunal where three more judges must review it. Only after two of those three judges agree with the decision is the decree of nullity of the marriage considered final.

In answer to your question, a judge of the tribunal actually makes the decision concerning the validity or invalidity of a marriage, but this decision is made within the framework of church law and is always reviewed by three judges of a second tribunal.

BRIAN R. CORMIER

35. ANNULMENTS FOR NON-CATHOLICS

My brother-in-law, who is Protestant, wants very much to join the Catholic Church. He was told by a priest that he cannot even begin instructions until his first marriage is annulled. Why is this necessary?

The priest wishes to delay instructions because your brother-in-law's previous marriage raises some doubts about the validity of his present union. Since your brother-in-law is not yet a Catholic, he would normally not share these doubts. To instruct him in the Catholic faith might very well disturb the sincerity of his judgment about this important matter.

Most likely, your brother-in-law's prior marriage was a sacramental one, i.e., a marriage between two baptized persons. The Church believes that such a marriage can be dissolved solely by the death of one of the spouses (canon 1141). It is not dissolved by a civil divorce. This attitude is not simply one of church law; it is a theological statement. A sacramental marriage symbolizes and participates in the mystery of Christ's union with the Church (cf. Eph. 5:25-33). Just as the Son of God permanently became one with humanity through his incarnation, so also Christian spouses become one body for life. Thus, in his debate with the Pharisees, Jesus points out: "What God has joined together, man must not separate. . . . Whoever divorces his wife and marries another commits adultery against her; so too, if she divorces her husband and marries another, she commits adultery" (Mark 10:9-12).

The Church takes this admonition very seriously. Still, it knows that many factors must be present to create the sacramental reality of matrimony, particularly the capacity of both persons to give of themselves fully, as Christ gave himself to us by assuming our humanity. If an essential element is missing in a marriage right from the start, it is considered invalid by the Church. Among the most important elements are the psychological readiness of the spouses to commit themselves to a deep interpersonal relationship and their ability to accept and carry out its important responsibilities.

Marriages are presumed to be valid until the contrary is clearly proven (canon 1060). A declaration of nullity is an official statement by an authoritative representative of the Church that a particular marriage, though originally presumed to be valid, has been conclusively shown to be invalid since it lacked some essential element from the very beginning. Since it is invalid, the marriage does not bind the parties for life, as had been originally thought.

If your brother-in-law's prior marriage is discovered to have been entered invalidly, the Church will no longer presume that he is bound by that union and will be able to recognize his present marriage as legitimate. If the Church's study of the situation proves to be negative, it would continue to look upon your brother-in-law's first marriage as valid and binding, and his present union as invalid. Your brother-in-law's internal assent to church teaching would bring with it the conclusion that he and his present spouse are involved in an irregular union. The priest who advised your brother-in-law was trying to clarify this perplexing situation prior to any formal commitment on his part.

JOHN A. ALESANDRO

36. ANNULMENT NOT WANTED

My daughter was divorced by her husband two years ago. She did not want the divorce. Can her former husband have the marriage annulled without her consent? Is there anything she can do to prevent the annulment?

Your daughter's situation is a very difficult one. If her former husband approaches the diocesan tribunal asking that their marriage be declared null, your daughter will be contacted and asked to take part in the process. Encourage her to do this and to state her views on the marriage clearly and openly, and also to register her objections to the annulment and her reasons for the objections. The tribunal personnel will be understanding of her position and will talk with her about her own feelings, the process and its implications.

Basically, what the tribunal is trying to do is come to a decision about the marriage presented to it for study. The task is a delicate one, to say the least, and every effort will be made to answer questions and allay fears so that the work done will benefit both parties and their lives within the church community. Regardless of who initiates the annulment inquiry, the rights of both parties are equal before church law.

If the tribunal, after considering all the information available, decides that the marriage is indeed null, a decision will be issued even though one party—in this case, possibly your daughter,—is not in favor of it. "Consent" to the annulment is not so much the issue, as what was the real truth of the matter. Was the marriage a true and valid marital commitment or not? The best way to ensure that this question is answered correctly is for both parties in the marriage to cooperate with the tribunal in honesty and openness.

Church law governing the annulment process is very careful to safeguard the rights of those in your daughter's position and requires that every decision rendered by a tribunal must be appealed to a second court. The actual operation of this appeal process differs from diocese to diocese, but your daughter should ask questions of the tribunal personnel and be sure she understands the process and knows how best to participate in it.

The bottom line to answer your question directly, is that the marriage can be annuled even if your daughter objects to it, but only when there is evidence and proof of nullity. Remember that the tribunal concerns itself with a very specific qustion: "Was the marriage valid or not?" and not "Who wants the annulment?" There are procedural steps required by law to ensure that this question is answered accurately and with objective fairness, but the process is not always able to meet everyone's personal needs or concerns.

ELISSA RINERE, C.P.

37. ANNULMENT DENIED

My brother's request for an annulment of his first marriage was just turned down. Does he have to leave the Church? He is already remarried.

No, he does not have to leave the Church and we certainly hope he would never want to.

A Catholic who has married validly, divorced and then married again without an annulment or special permission of the Church does have a problem. Basically, it is the problem of being objectively ineligible for receiving the sacraments of confession and Communion. Years ago the divorced and remarried Catholic was considered to be excommunicated—no longer a member of the church community—but this law has been abolished. Now, such a person remains a member of the Church by reason of baptism and retains many other rights and duties as a Catholic.

In most dioceses the Church has formed special groups for the divorced and remarried so that a loving pastoral care can be exercised toward them in their problems. By assisting at Mass, by good habits of prayer, by following Catholic practices in specifically Catholic Church groups, it is our hope that the divorced and remarried will not see themselves as cut off from the church family but rather an integral part of it. You should encourage your brother to contact his parish or diocesan office and inquire about these organizations and support groups.

Is this attitude a change from the past? You bet. It was born in Vatican II's teaching on the nature of God's mercy and the need for the Church to show that mercy to its own people, all of whom are sinners. Indeed, in a very real sense, the Church is compelled to this mercy if it has any hope at all of reflecting to the world the prodigal forgiveness of Jesus, the Lord.

THOMAS J. LYNCH

38. BILL OF RIGHTS

At a lecture I recently attended, the speaker referred to a section of the 1983 Code of Canon Law as a "Bill of Rights." Please explain what he meant by that reference.

The 1983 Code of Canon Law contains a new section on "The Obligations and Rights of all the Christian Faithful." It contains sixteen canons which list a series of rights and obligations which pertain to Catholics, regardless of whether they are clergy, religious or lay people. Most of these are drawn directly from statements in the documents of the Second Vatican Council.

When the Commission for the Revision of the Code began its work, many people encouraged them to include a statement of rights common to all Catholics in the new code. The idea took hold, and in the principles which the Commission adopted for the revision of the code the protection of rights was listed several times. The final product reflects the work of several study groups and comments received from bishops and scholars around the world.

The new listing of rights recognizes what has always been true of Catholics, namely that as baptized persons they have a common dignity and responsibility for building up the Body of Christ. Various rights and duties flow from their baptism and from their condition of membership in the Church.

Included in the so-called "Bill of Rights" in the new code are the obligations and rights to be in the communion of the Church, to grow in holiness, to spread the gospel, to work for justice and peace, and to assist the poor. Certain rights and obligations look to a Catholic's life within the Church, including obedience to church officials, the expression of desires, needs and personal opinion within the Church, reception of the spiritual goods of the Church such as the word of God and sacraments, etc. Some of the rights listed recall that basic human rights also belong within the Church, including the rights to form associations, to freedom from coercion in choosing a state in life, to a good reputation, and to privacy.

The listing also includes a statement that Christians can legitimately vindicate and defend their rights in the Church. Some have criticized the new code for not providing sufficient protection for the rights of Catholics in the Church, and this is one of the areas of church law which will undoubtedly see more attention in the future.

JAMES H. PROVOST

39. EASTERN RITE CHRISTIANS

What is an Eastern Rite and who is an Eastern Rite Catholic? Is a member of the Greek Orthodox Church considered a Catholic?

A rite is a group of faithful who are governed by laws and customs of their own based on ancient traditions, liturgy and law. These groups are acknowledged by the Holy See (Rome) as autonomous and distinct from each other. Often the various rites are called Eastern to distinguish them from the Latin (Roman) Rite. Some of the rites are the Alexandrine, Antiochene, Constantinopolitan, Chaldean, and Armenian. Many are in full communion with the Roman Catholic (Latin Rite) Church; these are known as Eastern Rite Catholics.

All the Eastern Rite Churches have common elements such as faith, sacraments and universal government. They also have differentiating elements such as liturgy (the most important element of a rite), canon law, and spiritual heritage.

Up until the middle of the 11th century the Catholic Church was the same throughout the world. It had its center in Rome under the authority of the Pope. In 1054, however, cultural, social and political factors led to a split (schism) between the Catholic Church in the West (Latin Rite) and the Catholic Church in the East (Eastern Rite). Some of the Eastern Rite faithful returned to full communion with the Catholic Church, remaining faithful to the Church of Rome and the Pope.

Those faithful who did not return to full communion continued in their own traditions. One such group are the Greek Orthodox. Since they did not reunite with the Church of Rome and the Pope after the Great Schism they are not Catholics in full communion. Since the Second Vatican Council however, great strides haves been made to bring about the full communion of the Greek Orthodox Church with the Roman Catholic Church.

BRIAN R. CORMIER

40. PRIESTS AND PUBLIC OFFICE

The Pope has said that priests are not supposed to hold public office. A priest in my town is running for mayor and the bishop is not stopping him. How is this possible?

The question of clerics holding public office is addressed in canon 285 of the 1983 Code of Canon Law. It states: "Clerics are prohibited from assuming those public offices which involve a participation in the exercise of civil power."

First of all, some public offices do not involve a participation in civil power—such would be a ceremonial mayor in a town where the council or manager has the real legislative and final power. A priest would be free to accept such an office in accord with church law.

Secondly, even if the office of mayor in your town is a position of legal authority, the bishop, if he were convinced that some extraordinary service could be rendered by a particular priest being mayor, could dispense the priest, that is, excuse him from the law in question and allow him to run. This would be unusual but legal since the Church has told its bishops that they may dispense from the disciplinary laws of the Church for a good and compelling reason.

Finally, the priest could ask the Holy See to grant him permission to run for office. If it were an unusual case where his candidacy would be helpful to all concerned, it might be allowed.

Generally speaking, for a priest to hold public office involving civil power is a disservice to the public and to the priesthood. It can and should be allowed under law only where unique and special circumstances make it needed and advantageous to both sectors.

THOMAS J. LYNCH

64

41. SISTERS AND BROTHERS IN PUBLIC OFFICE

I know there is a restriction for clerics, but where in the 1983 Code of Canon Law is it specified that religious sisters and brothers may not hold public office?

It is common and routine in composing legislation in the Church, as it is in American civil legislation, to avoid needless repetition of statutes by citing in one place canons found elsewhere in the law. This is called inclusion by reference. Indeed, the law would be intolerably cumbersome and unwieldy were it necessary to repeat laws in detail at every point where they were applicable.

A casual examination of the code will reveal how consistently this technique is used. It is called upon even more when the code deals with canonical structures similar to, but not identical with each other, as in the case of secular institutes or societies of apostolic life which are both forms of consecrated religious life in the Church. In these cases, the canons referred to may not exactly fit the situation in question and have to be applied as closely as possible.

Coming to the question posed, the relevant canon is 672, in which five canons from an earlier part of Book II which deals with clerics are "included by reference" in the law for all religious. The specific reference in this canon is to canon 285, which in its third section prohibits clerics from assuming public offices entailing a participation in the exercise of civil power, i.e., executive, legislative, or judicial power. The inclusion of canon 285, §3 into canon 672 has the effect of extending this prohibition to religious as well, without the need to repeat the earlier canon. "Religious are bound by the prescriptions of . . . can. 285. . . ." In light of this clear inclusion it cannot be said that canon 285 is addressed only to clerics. It is interesting to note that this same canon is again "included" in canon 739 and has the same effect for members of societies of apostolic life.

Finally, it should not be thought that canon 672 is new in the law of the Church and is thus something very contemporary. In the 1917 Code of Canon Law (the first code), canon 592 in the section on religious life "included by reference" nineteen canons from an earlier section which dealt with clergy. Among those canons was canon 139, §2, ". . . Clerics are not to assume public offices which carry with them the exercise of lay jurisdiction or administration." This applied to religious as well.

RICHARD A. HILL, S.J.

42. ANGLICAN PRIESTS BECOMING CATHOLICS

I recently read about an Anglican priest, married and with a family, who was ordained a Catholic priest. Please give some background on how and why this was done.

In the late 1970s several Episcopal priests approached officials of the Catholic Church with a desire to become Catholic priests. Their reasons were primarily personal, seeking to come to full communion in the Church. Many of these priests were married.

The Catholic officials recognized the personal spiritual reasons of these Episcopal priests, but they also saw the potential impact such a move would have within the Catholic Church because of its law on celibacy for priests, and on the developing ecumenical relations between Catholics and Episcopalians. So a careful study was conducted which resulted in approval by the American bishops and by the Vatican for each individual request to be evaluated by a special group of experts in the United States. The results are reviewed in the Vatican before permission is given for the Episcopal priest, after he has been received into full communion in the Catholic Church, to be ordained a Catholic priest.

The Catholic Church's law on celibacy means that those who are ordained may not marry, and that married persons may not be ordained priests. This is an ancient tradition in the Church, and became a general requirement for priests in the Catholic Church in the twelfth century. However, it is a church law, not a command from the Lord, and so the Church can dispense from it for serious reason. The spiritual welfare of the Episcopal priests has been considered sufficient reason to make individual exceptions to this canon law.

Such exceptions have been made in the past, but usually not in North America. The concern for the celibacy of priests has been such in this country that at the request of American bishops earlier in this century special rules were issued by the Vatican prohibiting Eastern Catholics from having married priests in North America, even though their canon law does permit married men to be ordained priests.

JAMES H. PROVOST

67

43. CONTEMPLATIVE NUNS

I am very upset over my daughter's plans to join an order of contemplative nuns. What do these orders do?

We are in a very special moment of the history of God's people. Pope John XXIII's vision is coming to fullness as we receive the fruits of the Second Vatican Council in a new Code of Canon Law. Inspired by the council and that great pope this new code richly describes and provides for the People of God.

First of all it affirms the basic equality of all God's people. All who have been baptized into Christ are his faithful (*Christifideles*) with equal dignity and rights and common obligations. But among God's people there are different offices or services and different states of life. One of these states is that of the consecrated life. The code tells us that

> The life consecrated through the evangelical counsels is a stable form of living, in which the faithful follow Christ more closely under the action of the Holy Spirit, and are totally dedicated to God, who is supremely loved. By a new and special title they are dedicated to seek the perfection of charity in the service of God's kingdom, for the honor of God, the building up of the Church and the salvation of the world. They are a splendid sign in the Church, as they foretell the heavenly glory (canon 573).

A later chapter which speaks about the apostolate of religious says first of all

> The apostolate of all religious consists primarily in the witness of their consecrated life, which they are bound to foster through prayer and penance (canon 673).

What will your daughter be doing? She will be seeking to follow Christ more closely, praying and doing penance for her own sins and the sins of us all. In her dedication and the gift of her life to the Lord she will be giving us a witness, she will be a clear sign to all that there is more than meets the eye that is of value, that God does exist and he is worth our all.

After the canon on the primary apostolate of all religious the Code adds one that speaks specifically of the apostolate of the contemplative institutes, such as your daughter seeks to join:

Institutes which are wholly directed to contemplation always have an outstanding part in the mystical Body of Christ. They offer to God an exceptional sacrifice of praise. They embellish the people of God with very rich fruits of holiness, move them by their example, and give them increase by a hidden apostolic fruitfulness (canon 674).

M. BASIL PENNINGTON, O.C.S.O.

44. DISPENSATION FROM VOWS

*My cousin just left the convent after 15 years. She says she was "dis-
pensed" from her vows. What does this mean? Is there any comparison
between this and a man leaving the priesthood?*

First of all, let me say that your cousin is undoubtedly in a difficult
period of transition. You will want to be as supportive as you can and,
of course, pray for her. She has made a very difficult decision and is
courageously carrying it through.

Like every other religious your cousin would have entered religious
life with high hopes and a wonderful life vision. She went through a
long probationary and preparatory period which lasted at the very
least four years and probably a good bit longer. Then, with all the joy
of a bride, she made a lifetime commitment to her Lord to follow him
closely in a particular way.

But life moves on. Things change. We change. One would expect
that once a lifetime commitment is made, everything would be settled.
But God is full of surprises. And we are full of weaknesses. What
particular combination of these come to play in a particular decision,
only God knows. "Judge not and you will not be judged." Our God has
said: "My ways are not your ways, nor my thoughts your thoughts, but
as high as is heaven above earth so are my ways beyond your ways and
my thoughts beyond your thoughts."

The Church has always recognized this and in the new Code of
Canon Law lays down the norm: "A perpetually professed religious is
not to seek an indult to leave the institute, except for very grave reasons,
weighed before the Lord." The commitment is to the Lord and it is
expected to be forever. But things can evolve. One must weigh things
honestly before the Lord always. He can ask one to move on. The
reason may be partly our fault. It can be due to our infidelity. That is
between the particular religious and the Lord. It can be because the
particular religious has gotten what God wanted the person to get out
of living in a particular institute and it is time to move on.

In any case, a religious can judge it is time to leave a religious
institute. He or she submits the request then to the judgment of the
Church. When the Church gives a religious permission to leave the
religious life or institute, "An indult to leave the institute, which is

lawfully granted and notified to the member, by virtue of the law itself carries with it . . . a dispensation from the vows and from all obligations arising from profession" (canon 692). Thus sister is "dispensed" from her vows.

Vows are promises made to God. God has said to his Church, to Peter and his successors, "Whatever you bind on earth is bound in heaven, whatever you loose on earth is loosed in heaven." In the Lord's name the Church can loose one from the promises made to God when there is a judgment that this is what the mercy and love of God calls for in this case. Then the one "dispensed" is free to move on to choose another path along which to walk with the Lord, whether it be in the partnership of marriage or in singleness. God's love is fully there. The call to holiness remains, for it is a call from the Lord to all the faithful. It is a matter of choosing a new way.

M. Basil Pennington, O.C.S.O.

45. FAST AND ABSTINENCE

What does the 1983 code say about fast and abstinence?

From the very beginning of Christianity we have been challenged to fulfill the gospel call to penance. Fasting—eating less than usual for some period of time—has always been acknowledged as one way to fulfill that call. Abstinence—staying away from one particular food—is a form of fasting.

The 1983 code specifically mentions these long-standing practices: "All. . . the Christian faithful in their own way are bound to do penance in virtue of divine law; . . . [they] are called in a special way to pray, exercise works of piety and charity and deny themselves by fulfilling their responsibilities more faithfully and especially by observing fasting and abstinence" (canon 1249).

In terms of specific legislation, the season of Lent and all Fridays throughout the year are penitential times in the Church. However, the exact rules for fasting and abstinence are regulated by the National Conference of Catholic Bishops.

The law has some norms. Abstinence from meat or some other food is to be recommended on the Fridays of the year. Fasting and abstinence are to be observed on Ash Wednesday and Good Friday (canon 1251). Everyone fourteen years of age and over is expected to observe the stipulated days of abstinence. Fasting is for those between the ages of eighteen and fifty-nine (canon 1252).

It is important to keep in mind that failure to observe a day of fast or abstinence does not necessarily constitute a sin. Age, illness or circumstances might make it necessary for an individual to employ other means to fulfill the gospel call to penance. Substantial failure to observe penitential times is, however, considered serious.

It would be well to point out here that one of the newer elements of the 1983 code is its broader approach to the whole topic of penance, of which fasting and abstinence are only a small part. The Christian faithful are encouraged to pray, to do works of charity and exercises of piety. Volunteer work in hospitals, visiting the sick, serving the needs of the aged and the lonely, instructing the young in the faith, participating as Christians in community affairs, meeting obligations to family, friends, neighbors, community, parish, are all activities which demand time, attention, concern and generosity. Our efforts to reach out to others in these ways can be very penitential and also very rewarding.

JOHN G. PROCTOR, JR.

46. CATHOLICS AND MASONS

Are Roman Catholics allowed to hold membership in Masonic organizations?

Generally, membership in any non-Catholic association which would serve in part or whole to oppose church authority or the teaching of the Church is forbidden. In this connection, the 1917 Code of Canon Law made explicit mention of Masonic associations. Its canon 2335 stated: "Those who join a Masonic sect or other societies of the same sort, which plot against the Church or against legitimate civil authority, incur excommunication." This seems like a harsh judgment against the Masonic tradition but in point of fact it was entirely warranted by the centuries old experience of the Church in Europe with Masonry. Unbiased history shows that European Masonry was indeed inimical to the Catholic Church. That this may not have entirely died out on the European scene is attested to by the scandal of the last decade in Italy when the famous P2 Lodge was charged by Italian authorities with subversive activities against both the civil state and the Catholic Church.

Our experience in the United States with transported Masonry is quite different. It would be difficult if not impossible to amass historical evidence that American Masonry of its very nature was or is anti-church or anti-state. In this country, Masonry has been primarily a fraternal and benevolent organization, rooted in insurance for its members and having its own ritual and lifestyle. In this it is not very much different from the Knights of Columbus, a parallel Catholic fraternal organization.

The 1983 Code of Canon Law does not mention Masonic associations explicitly but simply sums up the law by stating: "One who joins an association which plots against the Church is to be punished with a just penalty" (canon 1374). So your question can be answered with this general principle. Catholics are not allowed to hold membership in organizations, Masonic or otherwise, if those organizations are in fact anti-Catholic and plotting against the rights of the Church. Catholics may indeed hold membership in organizations, Masonic or otherwise, which are not basically anti-Catholic and do not plot against the Church.

It is clear that the Catholic Church would prefer its members to join and actively participate in those organizations which are distinctly

Catholic in nature and outreach. The distinctive doctrine and sacramental and spiritual benefits of such membership are not seen as readily available in other organizations. But when it comes down to the fundamental right of a Catholic to join a non-Catholic organization, that right is sustained in canon law as long as there is no question of membership which would violate the demands of morality or the basic rights of the Church itself.

Direction and guidance concerning the various organizations in your own locality can easily be obtained from the chancery office of your diocese.

THOMAS J. LYNCH

47. EXCOMMUNICATION

For what actions can a person be excommunicated? What are the effects of this punishment?

Excommunication is a serious penalty used by the Church to try to lead a sinner to reform and return to the proper living of a Christian life. It can be incurred only for serious sin.

For certain especially serious crimes the law itself imposes the penalty of excommunication. For example, excommunication is automatically incurred by someone directly involved in a completed abortion, or who commits the crimes of apostasy, heresy or schism. Some crimes are so serious that not only is an excommunication incurred automatically, but it cannot be lifted except by the Apostolic See. These are the crimes of desecrating the Blessed Sacrament, of using physical force against the pope, of a priest who attempts to absolve his accomplice in a sexual crime, of a bishop who consecrates someone a bishop without the mandate from the pope, or of a confessor who directly violates the seal of the confessional.

Although these excommunications can be incurred automatically, the person must at least know that some special penalty is attached to the crime in order actually to incur it. It can also happen that the crime becomes a public scandal; in these situations the bishop or a church judge can step in and make a public declaration that the person has already incurred the excommunication. This is not done very often, but it can be done in very serious cases.

For other crimes, the penalty of excommunication can be imposed if the matter is judged especially serious and the person is really not repentant. This requires the action of a church judge or another duly authorized official such as the diocesan bishop. A procedure must be followed to warn the person to repent, threatening excommunication if the person does not do so. If in fact the person fails to comply, then a second declaration has to be made to impose the excommuniction.

An excommunication prohibits the person from participating in the sacramental life of the Church or from discharging any offices, ministries or functions in the Church. If it is a situation where an automatic excommunication has also been declared publicly by a church official, or of an imposed excommunication after the special penal process has been followed, then more serious effects result. The person is to be physically excluded from liturgical celebrations, or these are to cease until the person leaves; the person cannot validly perform any actions of governance in the Church, and looses the right to any income from the Church.

Excommunications are healing or "medicinal" penalties. If the person repents and asks for forgiveness, the penalty must be lifted. Only certain officials in the Church are authorized to do this, mainly the diocesan bishop and certain people he designates, unless it is one of the five excommunications reserved to the Holy See. Excomunication does not throw someone out of the Church, but tries to lead the person back to the full living of a Catholic life.

James H. Provost

48. DIOCESAN SYNOD

Our bishop recently announced plans for a diocesan synod. What does this mean? Is it something that I can get involved in?

By reason of baptism, all the faithful carry out the three-fold mission of the Church by teaching, sanctifying and governing. The diocesan synod is a special exercise of the governing mission, in which a group of persons gathers for the purpose of legislating for the diocese. At the synod, laity, religious and clergy join the bishop in revising rules and regulations for the diocese.

The bishop consults with the priests' council to determine the advisability of holding a synod and then convenes it at his discretion. The law provides that certain key persons in the diocese must be called to the synod and laity, religious and clergy are represented in this provision. If the bishop wishes, he may also invite observers, i.e., church members or ministers not of the Roman Catholic faith.

By definition in church law, the synod is a consultative body. The participants make their ideas and opinions known on whatever diocesan matters are discussed, but the group does not have independent power to make new laws for the diocese. The bishop, as the legislator of the diocese, decides whether or not any norms proposed by the synod will be legally binding for the people.

Apart, however, from "lawmaking," a synod gives an entire diocese the opportunity to evaluate its effectiveness as a Christian community and to revitalize its efforts in witnessing the gospel. In this task, the synod requires the insights and talents of people from all areas of church life and ministry. If you do not have the opportunity for immediate involvement as a member of the synod, you will, I am sure, have an opportunity for secondary involvement through your parish. Your interest and concern will be a fine investment in the life of your local church.

ANN PREW-WINTERS

49. DIOCESAN PASTORAL COUNCIL

My husband has just been invited to be a member of the Diocesan Pastoral Council. What will he be asked to do as a member of this group?

The existence of the Diocesan Pastoral Council is a direct result of Vatican II (1962-1965). The bishops of the world assembled at that time affirmed and reaffirmed the fact that through baptism, laypersons have an indispensable role in the mission of the Church. The pastoral council is one result of this teaching. A bishop, by working with the pastoral council, is seeking suggestions and recommendations on matters which touch the pastoral activity of his entire diocese.

Canon law sets out some guidelines for how the council is to operate (canons 511-514), but basically the role and scope of the pastoral council is determined by the individual bishop. Members are appointed by him for a certain period of time and the code suggests that the lay membership of the council reflect the diverse population of the diocese: regions, economic and social conditions, professions, types of work.

The pastoral council acts in an ordinary capacity to advise the bishop; it enables him in his decision making to draw on the gifts and talents of others. When effectively organized and active within a diocese, it ensures a vital and life-giving relationship between pastoral policy and the daily Christian experience of the people. Through his appointment to the council, your husband has been presented with a unique opportunity to foster and strengthen this relationship and thus to enrich the entire diocese. Good luck to him!

DALE CALHOUN

50. PARISH COUNCILS

Why are there Parish Councils? Shouldn't the pastor be in charge of his own parish?

"To be or not to be, that is the question . . ." regarding parish councils. According to the 1983 Code of Canon Law, parish councils may come into being in a diocese if they are deemed necessary by the bishop after consulting the priest's senate. Optimistically the diocesan bishop will act in the spirit of the new Code of Canon Law which prompts the adoption of a new way of thinking about the Church and about the roles of all the faithful who are urged to participate in the mission of the Church according to their gifts.

Laity, according to the 1983 code, have a greater role to play in the life of the Church because all Christians share a basic equality through baptism and they are called to contribute to the building up of the local church which they call their parish: a particular community under the spiritual care of a pastor who is its proper shepherd. The laity serve on parish councils where representatives of the entire parish come together to take counsel with their pastor on the mission of the Church in that area.

The mission of the Church is to spread the message of Christ throughout the world. The clergy are not able to complete this mission without the cooperation of the laity and the laity are not able to fulfill their mission without the cooperation of the clergy. The parish council is one structure which allows for this mutual support and cooperation.

BRIAN R. CORMIER

51. PARISH COUNCILS AND CONFLICT

Our parish council is having a serious disagreement with the pastor. Each side is trying its best to be fair and open. What avenues of recourse are available for help in resolving the conflict?

Members of the church community have several avenues of recourse available to them for resolving conflict. We will concern ourselves with those avenues which keep the conflict within the community—and out of the courts.

The two main types of recourse are called "personal recourse" and "mediation recourse" (or just "mediation" for short). Before using either, the person who feels aggrieved by another person must first speak directly and privately with that other person. Perhaps this will clarify or correct the matter in the simplest way. But if it fails to prove satisfactory or is not practical, recourse provides an alternative to more formal measures (such as litigation).

Personal Recourse

Personal recourse is sometimes called "grievance process" or "hierarchical recourse." Simply stated, it involves taking the issue to the supervisor of the person with whom one is in conflict. This presumes a hierarchy of administrative levels.

Personal recourse is not always uniform among church structures, so it is especially important to consult the appropriate guidelines or to speak with someone in the bishop's office. Also, because not all church structures have worked out a procedure, personal recourse is not always available.

Mediation

Where personal recourse is not available or when it proves unsatisfactory, a person may make use of mediation. There are two kinds of mediation: conciliation and arbitration. The parties together can select either. Both processes are designed to reach a lasting settlement swiftly.

Conciliation is a negotiated settlement which the parties voluntarily agree to observe. It is the parties themselves who work out a compromise and plan of action to execute their agreement. The conciliator mediates dialogue between them, keeping the process moving without undue delay.

In arbitration the parties agree to refer their dispute to an impartial individual for settlement on the basis of information and arguments they present, and to accept the decision of the arbitrator as final and binding.

In your situation, "personal recourse" would mean going to the bishop as your pastor's next highest superior. Mediation would mean submitting the dispute to a conciliator or an arbitrator for settlement. Many dioceses have personnel available for these purposes and they would gladly be of service to you. Working through difficulties in this way can be a source of growth for all who take part in a spirit of openness and honesty.

ROGER A. KENYON

52. PARISH FINANCE COUNCIL

Our parish is in the process of setting up a finance board. What is its purpose and function?

The 1983 Code of Canon Law requires that in every parish there must be a finance council or committee. This is something that is new in our church law; the 1917 code did not make such a requirement.

It is a principle of the 1983 code that a group or foundation approved by the Church must have "its own finance council or at least two advisors, who according to the norm of its statutes assist the administrator in carrying out his or her function" (canon 1280). A legitimately established parish has this status, so canon 537 provides that "each parish is to have a finance council which is regulated by universal law as well as by norms issued by the diocesan bishop; in this council the Christian faithful, selected according to the same norms, aid the pastor in the administration of parish goods with due regard for the prescription of canon 532." Clearly this finance council is not a "board of directors" or a "board of trustees" to do business in the name of the parish. In the code, "the pastor represents the parish in all juridic affairs in accord with the norms of law; he is to see that the goods of the parish are administered in accord with the norms of canons 1281 and 1288" (canon 532). Those laws cited, canons 1281-1288, stipulate the duties which must be fulfilled by an administrator of church property.

It seems logical that considering the tasks involved, any prudent pastor would want to have the active participation of a competent finance council or committee to help him. For instance, among the duties of the finance council could be the preparation of a budget for the parish, and then a follow up on the success or failure of those who carry out that budget in daily parish functioning. The council might also advise on expenditures or investment plans. Whatever duties a finance council undertakes in a parish are, of course, determined according to the guidelines issued by the diocesan bishop.

The pastor has many duties: preaching the word of God and teaching Christian doctrine (canon 528, §1) various liturgical obligations (canon 528, §2); solicitude for all the Christian faithful in their various difficulties (canon 529, §1); and responsibility for seeing to it that the lay members of the Christian faithful understand their role in the mission of the Church not only at the parish level, but also at the diocesan and universal levels (canon 529, §2). If, in addition to these tremendous responsibilities, pastors were also solely responsible for every detail of temporal administration of the parish, the job would be that much more difficult. Certainly, this new parish structure is introduced as a help to the pastor and it presents another area of involvement for the people in the life of the local parish.

THOMAS G. DORAN

53. PARISH TEAM

In our diocese, the administration of a new parish has been given to a "designated team." What does this mean?

In the 1983 Code of Canon Law, canon 517 explains various ways in which the pastoral care of a parish can be exercised. These are given in addition to the traditional structuring of a parish with pastor and associate priests.

First, a parish or group of parishes can be entrusted to a team of priests. One is designated the moderator of the team, with responsibility to direct pastoral activity and to answer for it to the bishop. In this situation of *team ministry*, the priests are referred to as co-pastors.

Secondly, and in answer to your question, canon 517 allows for the pastoral care of a parish "to be entrusted to a deacon or to some other person who is not a priest or to a community of persons. . . ." In such a case, a priest would be assigned as the pastor and would act as a supervisor of the pastoral care being exercised by others. This new structure for parish ministry is often described as a *designated team* because the deacon or lay people involved are officially assigned or designated to participate in the pastoral care of the parish along with the pastor.

This is an important development in the life of the Church, and there seem to be two reason for it. On the one hand, there is the decline in the number of priests in active ministry and therefore the growing difficulty in many dioceses to staff parishes adequately. On the other hand, and on a completely different level of importance, there is the deepened awareness since Vatican II that all members of the Church share in its mission. Canon 204 summarizes this awareness very well by stating that all the Christian faithful, by reason of their baptism, are sharers in Christ's mission and therefore sharers in the mission which has been given to the Church.

MICHAEL H. GOSSELIN

54. PARISH PASTORAL WORKERS

One of the sisters working in our parish is listed on the bulletin as "associate pastor." I think only priests can be pastors, but my husband says, "Times have changed." Who is right?

It is true that for many things in the Church the times have changed, but "pastor" is not one of them. According to canon 519 of the 1983 Code of Canon Law, the parish priest is the proper pastor of the parish entrusted to him. He is responsible for the pastoral care of the people and carries out his duties with the cooperation of other priests, deacons and laypeople, according to the law.

Canon 517 mentions that where there is a shortage of priests the whole responsibility for pastoral care in a parish can be given over to deacons or lay people, but there must always be a priest appointed to the parish to direct the work done. Of course, this priest must be available for Mass and the administration of the sacraments, as his schedule allows. The possibility for deacons and lay people to be involved in total parish care is new in the law and can be pointed to as evidence that in this area, "times have changed." This change might also be part of what has given rise to the confusion you mention in your question.

For years in the United States the term "assistant" has been used for a priest assigned to a parish to work with the pastor. However, when lay people were hired to help with parish ministry, there were no commonly accepted titles to give them. Parishes were often free to choose their own terms and this has led to some inaccuracies and misunderstandings.

It is clear in the 1983 code that assistant or associate pastors in a parish must be priests. These titles are not correct for other workers in a parish. Perhaps the sister you mention would be better described as "pastoral associate," "pastoral team member," or "pastoral minister." These titles more accurately describe her position within the parish community.

MARY WALDEN, O.S.U.

55. PARISH RECORDS

What records do parish churches keep about parishioners?

Parishes are required by canon law (canon 535) to keep registers of baptisms, marriages, and deaths. Besides these, parishes in the United States generally also keep registers of confirmations and First Communions. Some pastors keep a record of their sick calls for their own future use and information.

Once a person has been baptized or has made a profession of faith in the Catholic Church, the law requires that a notation be made in the baptismal register of any change in the person's status in the Church. Thus the individual's baptismal record will also contain notice of confirmation, marriage, adoption, ordination, profession as a religious brother or sister, change of rite, nullity of marriage, laicization, or dispensation from religious vows. Other parishes or church agencies are required to notify the church of baptism of these events.

When a couple is to be married, church law (canon 1067) requires prudent investigation about their status, freedom, and readiness. The various documents used for this investigation, as well as any necessary dispensations or other pertinent papers, are all kept in the permanent marriage file of the parish.

The pastor must strive to know the members of the parish (canon 529), and many pastors find that an updated census is an indispensable tool for attaining that knowledge. An ordinary census card contains information about each member of a family or household, such as full names, places and dates of birth, status (as we discussed above), educational background, special interests, parish involvements, and financial contributions. An increasing number of parishes around the country are computerizing this information.

As the legal representative of the parish and the administrator of parish property and finances (canon 532), the pastor is required to keep accurate records of income and expenditures (canon 1284, 7°). The methods of record keeping are not specified in the universal law, but virtually all parishes in the United States keep week-by-week records of individual members' contributions, both for the information of the

87

parish as well as for the benefit of the parishioner when tax time rolls around.

Parish records about parishioners are confidential, and their primary purpose is, as we have said, to indicate the current status of the individual in the Church. Even the older parish registers are to be preserved carefully, and such records are of great interest to historians and genealogists, since they frequently contain information that cannot be found elsewhere. Nonetheless, they remain essentially private records, and access to them is left to the discretion of the individual pastor.

DENNIS W. MORROW

56. PREACHING IN CHURCH

Is it correct that only a priest or deacon can preach in church?

The 1983 Code of Canon Law is remarkable for its greatly enhanced recognition of the laity's role in the Church. The 1983 code specifies many of the rights and duties of lay people in Church. In canons 224-231, some of these rights and duties are outlined. Lay persons have both the obligation and the right to acquire a knowledge of Christian doctrine adapted to their capacity and condition so that they can live in accord with that doctrine. The laity are to announce this doctrine and to defend it when necessary. They are to be well equipped to assume their role in exercising the apostolate. The issue of preaching must be treated in this context of the laity's obligation to announce and defend Christian doctrine.

Canon 766 states: "Lay persons can be admitted to preach in a church or oratory if it is necessary in certain circumstances or if its useful in particular cases according to the prescriptions of the conference of bishops. . . ." There is one important exception to this general rule. The homily, as part of the liturgy, is reserved to a priest or deacon. Furthermore, as the canon states, general norms about lay preaching are to be drawn up by the episcopal conference, in our case, the National Conference of Catholic Bishops.

It is particularly important to note the code's very broad understanding of the term *preaching.* Formal preaching and catechetical formation are prime examples of proclaiming Christian teaching and doctrine. But other means are also explicity mentioned: the exposition of doctrine in schools, academies, conferences and meetings of every type; public declarations made by legitimate authority on the occasion of certain events; press coverage; and all instruments of social communication.

Finally, it is necessary to make a few remarks about the ecclesial nature of preaching. Preaching is a formal act done in the name of the Church. In the 1917 code, preaching was seen as a specific act of jurisdiction because it was understood to bind the consciences of those who listened. There is a different nuance to the present code's understanding of preaching, but also emphasized is its ecclesial nature. Thus, the code says that the first purpose of preaching is "to propose those things which one ought to believe and do for the glory of God and for the salvation of humankind" (canon 768). Preaching is also to communicate the Church's teaching about the dignity and freedom of the human person; the unity and stability of the family and its duties; the obligations which men and women have from being joined together in society; and the ordering of temporal affairs according to God's plan (canon 768, §2). Above all, preaching is to be accomplished in a manner accommodated to the condition of the listeners and adapted to the needs of the times.

JOHN G. PROCTOR, JR.

57. COMMISSIONING LECTORS

Our parish wanted to have a commissioning service for our new lectors but the pastor said that the women lectors could not be included. Is he correct?

There has been a lot of confusion about the "commissioning" of lectors because of the special lay ministry of lectors for which only men can be installed. A parish commissioning, however, is not the same as an installation of permanent lectors, so is not subject to the same canonical restrictions. Let me explain.

Several years ago Pope Paul VI did away with what were known as "minor orders," steps on the way to becoming a priest, and in their place he introduced two new "ministries" open to lay people. They were lector and acolyte. These were not the same as the occasional serving of Mass in a parish church or reading the Scriptures during Mass. Instead, they were permanently installed ministers who in addition to what Mass servers do (for acolytes) or reading Scripture during Mass (for lectors), would also be involved in preparing people to do this part time and would carry on other duties in the Church.

In keeping with past tradition, the pope restricted these new lay ministries to lay men. But this did not restrict women from serving, for example, as lectors on the parish level. Indeed, the revised norms for Mass permitted bishops to determine the involvement of women in doing the readings at Mass, even within the sanctuary.

Today the usual practice has been to install as permanent lectors only those who are preparing for ordination either as permanent deacons or on the way to becoming a priest. The bishop is the one who installs such lectors.

In parishes, lay people continue to provide the important service of reading at Mass. These are considered temporary lectors; they have not made a life-long commitment to this, as an installed lector does. If they are commissioned, it is not the same as the installation of a lector; rather, it is a ceremony within the parish to recognize the important service these people are doing in the community for the coming months.

Obviously, the pastor has an important voice in what ceremonies will take place in the parish. If the pastor determines there is good reason not to commission the women lectors, it may be that no commissioning ceremony would be appropriate at this time. This does not stop lay men and women from providing the service of readers, however, as commissioning is not needed in order to do this.

JAMES H. PROVOST

58. FIRING CATHOLIC SCHOOL TEACHERS

May Catholic schools terminate lay teachers for failure to conduct their personal lives in accordance with church teachings? For example, may a Catholic school terminate a teacher who has had an abortion?

While there has been surprisingly little judicial scrutiny of this specific question, there are several cases in American civil law in which a judge has expressed the view that a sectarian school may prescribe a code of moral conduct that its teachers must follow. Under these holdings, a Catholic school would be permitted to terminate a teacher who violated the school's prohibition against faculty members having an abortion.

However, a sectarian school may not enforce its code of moral conduct in a manner which would discriminate on the basis of race, sex, or national origin. For example, terminating a lay teacher who becomes pregnant out of wedlock may run afoul of the law if it is shown that the school does not similarly terminate male teachers who engage in premarital sex, and terminating a female teacher who has an abortion may be unlawful if similar action is not taken against a male teacher who requests his wife to have an abortion.

PETER M. SHANNON, JR.

59. TAX EXEMPTION FOR CHURCH PROPERTY

In our small town, a large parcel of land has been bought by the diocese. Will this property be exempted from the property tax, and if so, is the authority for this exemption drived from canon law or civil law?

Property tax exemptions for real estate owned by religious organizations are authorized by state statute, not canon law. Such exemptions are generally allowed to all charitable organizations which own real estate. Exemptions, however, are normally allowed only for property used by the religious or charitable organization for its exempt purpose.

Thus, if a diocese purchased a large tract of land in a small town and used the land to build a religious school or church, the land would be exempt from the property tax. However, if the land were used for a farming venture or for some other income producing activity unrelated to the diocese's religious purpose, the property would not be exempt.

This exemption for property used by religious and charitable organizations grew out of the tradition of religious freedom in America. The exemption continues today in most, if not all states, and has been upheld by the courts as allowed by the First Amendment of the United States Constitution.

PETER M. SHANNON, JR.

60. WHERE TO GO FOR MORE HELP

If I had a question about church law or procedure and this booklet was not available to me, where could I go to get accurate answers and information?

The first place to look for an answer to a question about church law is in the Church's book of laws: The Code of Canon Law. The 1983 code is up to date, readable, available in English, and covers all the broad general principles of the rights and responsibilities of God's people. It should be available in the religion section of your public library or can be purchased at your Catholic bookstore. You don't have to be a canon lawyer to understand it, although formal training would be needed when it comes to precise interpretation. Also, wouldn't it be fun to ask your pastor after Mass: "Father what do you think about canon 212, §3?"

If you are not the "do it yourself" type, your parish rectory should be your first stop. Most questions of law and practice, whether general to the whole Church or local to your own diocese, can be answered with clarity and completeness by parish priests.

Should the topic be a bit more intricate, the Chancery Office (sometimes called Pastoral Center or Bishop's Office) of your diocese is a good bet. Every diocesan chancery has qualified personnel who would be able to help you. Over the years they have developed skills in the sensitive and authentic interpretation of laws which is something really different from simply knowing the letter of the law.

If your question is directly related to the annulment of marriage, then you should write or call your diocesan tribunal. Every diocese has one. Often it is housed along with or quite near the chancery. Tribunal personnel are also formally trained in canon law.

Should all these avenues for some strange reason be unavailable, then you should write to: Canon Law Society of America, Catholic University, Washington DC 20064. This is the headquarters for the C.L.S.A., the professional society for American canonists. Its membership and leadership are uniquely equipped to bring a depth of scholarship and a wealth of practical experience to bear upon questions of the law.

A final prayer for those who have written or read these columns: May our search and inquiry into the Church's law lead us to Jesus Christ and His supreme law that we truly love Him and one another!

THOMAS J. LYNCH

AUTHORS

John A. Alesandro, J.C.D., is chancellor of the Diocese of Rockville Centre, New York.

Dale Calhoun, J.C.L., is vice-officialis of the Diocese of Yakima, Washington.

Brian R. Cormier, J.C.L., is vice-officialis of the Diocese of Worcester, Massachusetts.

Thomas G. Doran, J.C.D., is vicar general for the Diocese of Rockford, Illinois.

Otto L. Garcia, J.C.D., is chancellor of the Diocese of Brooklyn, New York.

William F. Gold is pastor of Saint Margaret Church in Oceanside, California.

Michael H. Gosselin, J.C.L., is a judge on the Metropolitan Tribunal of the Archdiocese of Hartford, Connecticut.

Richard A. Hill, S.J., J.C.D., is associate professor of canon law at the Jesuit School of Theology in Berkeley, California.

John M. Huels, O.S.M., J.C.D., is associate professor of canon law at the Catholic Theological Union in Chicago, Illinois.

Roger A. Kenyon, J.C.D., is associate director of the Metropolitan Tribunal in the Archdiocese of Seattle, Washington.

Ellsworth Kneal, J.C.D., is directing judge of the Metropolitan Tribunal for the Archdiocese of Saint Paul and Minneapolis, Minnesota.

Thomas J. Lynch, J.C.L., is chancellor of the Archdiocese of Hartford, Connecticut.

Paul S. Loverde, J.C.L., is associate judicial vicar for the Diocese of Norwich, Connecticut.

Dennis W. Morrow, J.C.L., is archivist for the Diocese of Grand Rapids, Michigan.

M. Basil Pennington, O.C.S.O., J.C.L., is a monk of Saint Joseph's Abbey in Spencer, Massachusetts.

Joseph N. Perry, J.C.L., is judicial vicar for the Archdiocese of Milwaukee, Wisconsin.

Edward G. Pfnausch, J.C.L., is assistant judicial vicar of the Archdiocese of Hartford, Connecticut.

Ann Prew-Winters, J.C.L., is associate director of the tribunal in the Archdiocese of Cincinnati, Ohio.

John G. Proctor, J.C.L., is vice-officialis of the Diocese of San Diego, California.

James H. Provost, J.C.D., is associate professor of canon law at The Catholic University of America in Washington, D.C.

John A. Renken, J.C.D., S.T.D., is vice-chancellor and vice-officialis for the Diocese of Springfield in Illinois.

Elissa Rinere, C.P., J.C.L., is a defender of the bond on the Metropolitan Tribunal of the Archdiocese of Hartford, Connecticut.

Peter M. Shannon, Jr., J.D., J.C.L., is a member of the firm of Keck, Mahin and Cate in Washington, D.C.

Royce R. Thomas, J.C.L., is chancellor and vice-officialis of the Diocese of Little Rock, Arkansas.

Mary Walden, O.S.U., M.A., is pastoral associate at Saint Rita parish in Saint Louis, Missouri.

Lawrence G. Wrenn, J.C.D., is judicial vicar of the Matrimonial Appeals Court for the Province of Hartford, Connecticut.

INDEX

Numbers are page numbers

99

Numbers are page numbers

Numbers are page numbers

Numbers are page numbers

Numbers are page numbers